MW01172123

God In My Life

Remembering God's Work In The Military, The Ministry, And The Messiness Of Life

Chaplain Rich Young

Copyright © 2024 by Rich Young

All rights reserved. No part of this publication may be reproduced, distributed, or transmitted in any form or by any means, including photocopying, recording, or other electronic or mechanical methods, without the prior written permission of the publisher, except in the case of brief quotations embodied in critical reviews and/or certain other noncommercial uses permitted by copyright law.

Chaplain Rich Young
Email: chaplainrichyoung@gmail.com

Book layout by Sam Wright
Cover layout by Rob Williams
Cover photo by Rich Young: The author conducts a worship service for U.S. Army soldiers while deployed to the Iraqi desert in 1991.

God In My Life / Rich Young – 1st Edition
ISBN: 9798325500954

All Bible verses are quoted from the English Standard Version (ESV).

Greeting Card credit: © DaySpring Cards, Inc. Used by permission.

TABLE OF CONTENTS

Foreword

I am so proud of my dad for writing this book. As you will read in these pages, this is his life. It is personal, it is vulnerable, and it is authentic. I have watched many of these chapters unfold from my front-row seat, and it has been a privilege to do so — even getting pulled into the story on occasion.

We were sitting at breakfast one morning during a quiet weekend in Virginia, my extended family all together, when I first mentioned to my parents about publishing these memoirs. I was happy that they would hear me out, and even more happy that they would engage with me on it. By the end of the day, after a few planning discussions and roping my brother into the conversation, we were on our way.

There are a few reasons why I wanted us to do this. I wanted to record the stories that my dad experienced in his seven decades of life. Often people think of this too late, but I hoped we still had time. I wanted to enjoy this process with my dad and my brother. Our lives have separated us geographically since childhood, and this would be a way to keep us connected. And, most of all, I wanted to honor the legacy of a man who held many roles in my life: father, mentor, pastor, role model and best friend.

Thank you for enjoying these pages with us. I pray you will feel inspired and moved by what you read, just like I was.

-Casey Young

Introduction

Reading through the Psalms in 2001 while at Fort Leavenworth, Kansas, I ran across a passage that spoke to me and gave me an idea. The passage was Psalm 78:4-7:

"We will not hide them from their children; we will tell the next generation the praiseworthy deeds of the LORD, his power, and the wonders he has done.
5 He decreed statutes for Jacob and established the law in Israel, which he commanded our forefathers to teach their children,
6 so the next generation would know them, even the children yet to be born, and they in turn would tell their children.
7 Then they would put their trust in God and would not forget his deeds but would keep his commands."

The idea came to me, that I sincerely hope is from the Lord, to record the things in my life the Lord has done that can only be attributed to Him. There is absolutely no way I can remember all of them.

One purpose of documenting God's work in my life is that I might tell "the praiseworthy deeds of the LORD" (Verse 4) so they might be passed on to future generations. Not only do I want our sons Casey and Kelly to know the God of their father, but I also want our grandsons Braden and Ashton and their children's children (Verse 7) to know Him too. So, in my own small way, I hope to contribute and be used by the Lord in bringing future generations of Youngs into a saving knowledge of Jesus Christ.

A second, but related, purpose is for these testimonies to be signs that point to Jesus. I mean for no attention to be drawn to me. I do pray they will point to Him and serve as examples of what a gracious and loving Shepherd of his sheep He is.

A third reason is that you might be encouraged by reading them. He has been faithful to Sandy and me in some unbelievable ways. He is an immutable God and will be equally faithful to you as well.

The fourth and final reason is to encourage you to likewise document His work in your own life. My conviction is that the spiritual discipline of remembering is too often neglected in the church today. And yet the idea is so prominent in the Bible. Here are a few examples:

When God gave Moses the Ten Commandments, He wanted them to remember that He was their deliverer—the One who rescued them from slavery in Egypt. The preamble to the Ten Commandments begins "And God spoke all these words, saying, 'I am the LORD your God, who brought you out of the land of Egypt, out of the house of slavery.'" (Exodus 20:1-2)

Joshua set up 12 memorial stones from the middle of the Jordan River to help future generations remember that God caused the Jordan to stop flowing so the Israelites might cross into the Promised Land on dry ground. Joshua 4:1-7 explains it like this:

"When all the nation had finished passing over the Jordan, the LORD
said to Joshua, 2"Take twelve men from the people, from each tribe a man,
3and command them, saying, 'Take twelve stones from here out of the midst of the Jordan, from the very place where the priests' feet stood firmly, and bring them over with you and lay them down in the place
where you lodge tonight.'" 4Then Joshua called the twelve men from the
people of Israel, whom he had appointed, a man from each tribe. 5And
Joshua said to them, "Pass on before the ark of the LORD your God into the midst of the Jordan and take up each of you a stone upon his shoulder,
according to the number of the tribes of the people of Israel, 6that this
may be a sign among you. When your children ask in time to come, 'What
do those stones mean to you?' 7then you shall tell them that the waters of the Jordan were cut off before the ark of the covenant of the LORD. When it passed over the Jordan, the waters of the Jordan were cut off. So, these stones shall be to the people of Israel a memorial forever."

We also see the significance of remembering when we look at the Lord's Supper. Luke 22:19 tells us, "And he took bread, and when he had given thanks, he broke it and gave it to them, saying, 'This is my body, which is given for you. Do this in remembrance of me.'" Paul says it like
this in his letter to the Corinthian church: 23"For I received from the Lord

what I also delivered to you, that the Lord Jesus on the night when he was betrayed took bread, [24]and when he had given thanks, he broke it, and said, 'This is my body, which is for you. Do this in remembrance of me.' [25]In the same way also he took the cup, after supper, saying, 'This cup is the new covenant in my blood. Do this, as often as you drink it, in remembrance of me.' [26]For as often as you eat this bread and drink the cup, you proclaim the Lord's death until he comes."

Jesus wanted us not only to remember what He did on the cross for His people, but to be fed spiritually and encouraged by remembering what He had done.

One of my favorite biblical examples of remembering what God had done is the well-known story of David and Goliath found in 1 Samuel 17. After Saul tried to dissuade David from fighting Goliath, David (who we know was a shepherd) said to Saul in verses 34-36, "Your servant used to keep sheep for his father. And when there came a lion, or a bear, and took a lamb from the flock, I went after him and struck him and delivered it out of his mouth. And if he arose against me, I caught him by his beard and struck him and killed him. Your servant has struck down both lions and bears, and this uncircumcised Philistine (Goliath) shall be like one of them, for he has defied the armies of the living God."

David, when facing a difficult challenge, looked back and remembered what God had done in the past and, by doing so, was encouraged and strengthened to face what was ahead of him.

With all this biblical encouragement and examples to remember, I hope you will do the same in your life. Work to develop the spiritual discipline of remembering what God has done in your life—in particular those things that can only be attributed Him. Then you will be able to "tell the next generation the praiseworthy deeds of the LORD, his power, and the wonders he has done. . . so the next generation would know them, even the children yet to be born, and they in turn would tell their children. Then they would put their trust in God and would not forget his deeds but would keep his commands."

Chapter 1: More Than Existing November 7, 1971

Be a Marine and get a Marine tattoo! Those were my two goals in life as I grew up. My dad was a Marine noncommissioned officer in the South Pacific during World War II and, following the war, often attended special celebrations to honor military veterans. He frequently took me along. The Marine Corps was an integral part of dad becoming the man he was. I wanted to be like him, so I enlisted in the Marine Corps after high school to pursue my dream.

During my first year in the Corps, I noticed something missing in my life. I always had to be looking forward to something like payday, the weekend or going home to be with my girlfriend. I couldn't get up and say, "Today is worth living. There is a purpose for me today." This empty feeling increased when I was assigned to Iwakuni, Japan, in 1971. The thought in my mind was, "Rich, you aren't really living—all you're doing is existing." Shortly after arriving in Iwakuni, I met a fellow Marine named Jerry who began telling me about Jesus. He showed me John 10:10 and the words of Jesus spoke to me: "I came that they may have life and have it abundantly." It seemed as though Jesus was offering to give me something that was 180 degrees different from what I was experiencing. With His words lingering in my mind, I continued to reflect on what they might mean and what an abundant life might be like. I began attending chapel with Jerry.

I started off very well in the Marines; graduating first in my class in school, I was promoted to lance corporal after only three days as a private first class. Then an event took place that jeopardized my "good Marine" status and made me look even deeper inside myself. Having scored three touchdowns in an intramural football game victory, I headed to the bars in Iwakuni to celebrate with friends. After having a few drinks, I realized I was on duty and wasn't even allowed to be off base. I still remember catching a Japanese cab back to my little Quonset hut on base, hoping and praying the whole way that I wouldn't get caught. I knew I could face disciplinary charges and could even get busted.

The next day, Nov. 7, 1971, I went to an evening chapel service with Jerry. Sitting in the chapel pew during the service, I silently prayed, "Jesus, if you'll give me an abundant life, I want it." While I understand that what I experienced doesn't happen to everyone, I immediately had a sense of forgiveness and cleanliness I'd never experienced before. I knew I'd become a Christian!

Not only did my life change that night, but so too did my eternity. I discovered there was more to life than payday, intramural sports or being with my girlfriend. My life now had purpose and meaning. I knew God loved me. I knew He would never leave me, and that I was His for eternity. I knew I had been forgiven and that God no longer held my sin against me—all because of what Jesus did on the cross. I started experiencing the truth and power of His Word. I learned that He really is who He says He is in His Word. And, on top of all that, I will spend forever in a place where all tears will be wiped away and "death shall be no more, neither shall there be mourning, nor crying, nor pain anymore, for the former things have passed away." (Revelation 21:4) I now knew what Jesus meant when He promised me abundant life—I was living it!

Marine Corps Basic Training
Parris Island, SC
October 1970

Chapter 2:
My Call Into The Ministry
1972-1974

As I mentioned, I became a Christian in November of 1971. Five or six months later, I was given the opportunity to preach my first sermon. It was in downtown Iwakuni at a missionary's place. The name of the missionary was Reverend Ray Pedigo, and the name of the ministry was the Iwakuni Evangelistic Center (IEC). Reverend Pedigo was an American missionary who traveled the various islands of Japan preaching the Gospel; Iwakuni was his home base in Japan.

I would go, along with several other Marines, to IEC a couple times a week. On Friday evenings we taught English to Japanese high school students by using the Good News for Modern Man version of the Bible. Sunday afternoons we would meet with some of the same high schoolers for a church service. I was asked to preach one Sunday and did so gladly—but fearfully, too. My text was the story of the Prodigal Son from Luke 15. I would say a few sentences, then a translator would translate what I said. Much to my surprise, two or three of the kids wanted to accept the Lord when I finished. I was so surprised that I didn't know what to do or say. I don't remember what I did do, but I hope I had enough spiritual maturity to at least lead them in prayer and talk to them about following Jesus.

On another occasion, I was the lay reader one Sunday morning in a chapel service out on base. I think the chapel's name was the Wing Side Chapel. After reading Scripture one morning, at least one person (and maybe more) commented to me about how well I had done and what a good speaking voice I had. I had certainly never thought of that, especially since giving a speech in high school scared me half to death.

My desire to go into the ministry began not long after that. It was just something I wanted to do. I also began to sense the Lord was leading me in that direction.

So, when I thought about it, the following things seemed to have fallen into place:

1. The Lord had blessed my ministry at the Iwakuni Evangelistic Center.
2. Folks told me I was good at it (gifts and/or talents confirmed by the Body of Christ).
3. I had a deep desire to do it.

All these things caused me to believe the Lord was leading me in that direction.

Iwakuni Evangelistic Center
Iwakuni, Japan
1972

Chapter 3: God's Peace In A Dental Chair 1973

One of my first—and very real—experiences with the peace of God came when I was having my wisdom teeth removed. One or two of them had been pulled when I was in Japan; the others were to be removed at South Weymouth Naval Air Station in Massachusetts. I was quite nervous about the whole ordeal.

I remember getting into the dentist's chair and the dental tech asked me if I'd like to look at a *Playboy* magazine while I waited. I declined his offer. It wasn't long until the peace of God literally seemed to flood my soul. I remember sitting in the chair with peace and joy that I don't believe I had ever experienced before. All nervousness was gone, and I did the best I could to watch what he was doing by looking at the reflection in his glasses. What Paul said to the Philippians is indeed true—God gives peace that passes all understanding.

Chapter 4: Marine On A Four-Day Work Week? 1974

I began to sense God leading me into the ministry while stationed at South Weymouth, Massachusetts. I was on what the Marine Corps called an instructor and inspector assignment, meaning we worked with Marine Corps reservists. Because reservists have civilian jobs, they did their Marine Corps training one weekend a month and two weeks during the summer. That being the case, my work week during this period was Wednesday through Sunday.

It was during this time that God did something totally unbelievable. I met Bill Bell, a Navy corpsman and a Christian. Bill was serving as the pastor at an Assemblies of God church plant in Hull, Massachusetts. He asked me about working with him there. I told him I could help on Sunday evenings and possibly during the week, but not on Sunday mornings because I would be working with the reservists.

All my fellow Marines at work, including my captain, knew I was a Christian and planned to go Bible college to prepare for the ministry after being discharged from the Marine Corps. Thinking the obvious answer would be "no," I went to my captain and asked if I could have Sundays off to work at the church with Bill. Surprisingly, he said I could, meaning I only worked four days a week for the last several months I was in the Marine Corps.

What a confirmation of God's blessings on my life!

Chapter 5: Your Wife Will Be A Fruitful Vine September 28, 1974

I returned from Iwakuni on Aug. 25, 1972. Sandy and I were married eight days later on September 2. Sandy was not a Christian, and I had been a Christian for about 10 months. There is no way to rationalize that marrying a non-Christian was OK; it was blatant disobedience to the Lord on my part. God is both sovereign and gracious, however, and showed Himself to be faithful in our marriage and in Sandy's eventual salvation.

I had two years left in the Marine Corps when we got married. Sandy graduated from the Jameson Hospital School of Nursing in New Castle, Pennsylvania, on April 13, 1973. She came to live with me in Massachusetts that night after graduation.

I was discharged from the Marine Corps in August of 1974 and began attending South Eastern Bible College (SEBC) in September of that year. My friends at my church in Massachusetts had been praying for Sandy's salvation, as had my new friends at SEBC. They were all great support to me as I struggled to live with a non-Christian wife. Among those friends were Virginia Chadwick, Ray and Jeannie Gilliard, and Alice and Henry Higginbotham.

I was extremely convinced that the Lord was directing me into the ministry. I had no idea what He was going to do, since not many congregations are interested in a pastor whose wife isn't a Christian and won't even go to church. I was confident, however, that He would do something. I spent more time in prayer during college and seminary than during any other time in my life; most of the prayer focused on Sandy's salvation, although later in seminary it also focused on God's direction in my life after graduation with a non-Christian wife. I don't remember now how much time I spent in prayer and fasting, but I do remember on one occasion fasting for a week while I prayed for Sandy.

God confirmed His call on my life on Sept. 28, 1974—my first month at SEBC. Sandy had gone to work, and I was at home in our campus apartment by myself. I took some time in the afternoon and was praying for her to come to know Christ in her life. I then had an experience I've only had a few times in my life. I randomly opened my Bible immediately after prayer and the very first words I saw were:

Your wife will be like a fruitful vine in your house. Psalm 128:3

The words spoke to me in a very real way, a way that was much more than just wishful thinking. I immediately had tears in my eyes and began sobbing. I was sure it was the Holy Spirit giving me a promise that Sandy would one day become a Christian. I knew God had spoken to me that day.

I held on to that promise for 12 or 13 years until Sandy got saved. It was that promise from God that really kept me going through some difficult years and tough times in our marriage. When there were times I wanted to give up, throw in the towel and forget about the ministry, it was that promise that gave me the strength to continue preparing for what I felt God had called me to do.

Exactly when Sandy became a Christian is unknown, except to God. It was sometime while we were stationed at Schofield Barracks, Hawaii, between 1984 and 1987. Since that time, she has become a dedicated student of the Scriptures, grown, matured, had her own fruitful ministry and has, indeed, become a fruitful vine within my house.

Our Wedding Day
Ellwood City, PA
September 2, 1972

Chapter 6: My Birthday Card From God June 1976

My college years were difficult. Sandy was working at Polk General Hospital in Bartow, Florida, and I was a door-to-door solicitor for the *Tampa Tribune*. I was overly involved in Westside Assembly of God in Auburndale, Florida. At the time, I was also going to school full-time and putting in a lot of hours studying. We didn't have much time together, were living in two different worlds when we did have time together, didn't have any money and just plain didn't get along well at all.

One of the darkest times for me was during the spring of 1976. Besides all of the above, I sprained my ankle running back to the car in the rain one evening after peddling newspapers. Sandy took me to the Winter Haven Emergency Room the next morning, and I was wheeled out with a swollen, sprained ankle and crutches. Never having been on crutches before, I did not realize that the unpadded hand rests caused blisters. So, after a few days on crutches, I ended up with huge blisters on both hands.

Not only could I not walk, but I also couldn't carry my young son Casey because of the blisters. I had had about all I could take—I was really wondering if it was worth it to serve the Lord and to prepare for the ministry that I thought He had called me to. I had no money, an unsupportive wife, a marriage that was falling apart, I couldn't walk or hold anything, and I was very discouraged, maybe even depressed.

My birthday was coming in a couple of months, and I remember hoping something good would happen to me for my birthday. Sandy got me a $5.00 pair of Kmart tennis shoes because that was all we could afford.

Then, at the beginning of June, I went to the mailbox and took out a birthday card. I read the words and began to get tears in my eyes. I then read the words again and began to cry like a baby. The Lord had definitely spoken to me through the words of my birthday card.

God Holds Your Hand

God understands the way you take.
He knows the trials of each day,
And sympathizing lends an ear
To hear you e'en before you pray.
He walks with those who trust His love,
He holds them by the hand to guide,
What need to fear or be dismayed
With His dear Presence by your side!
"He knoweth the way that I take;
when he hath tried me,
I shall come forth as gold." (Job 23:10)

I can't explain the encouragement I got from that card. All of a sudden, I knew I was not forgotten and that God remembered me. He knew where I was, what I was feeling and everything I was going through. I knew He was there with me, and that things would be OK.

I then looked down to see who had sent me the card. It was blank—no one had signed it. It was my birthday card from God!

I did check the postmark and discovered my Grandma Young in Miami had sent the card. She had no idea, however, what I was going through or experiencing at the time. I still consider it my birthday card from God. I've kept the birthday card in my Bible ever since.

My Birthday Card From God
June 8, 1976
© DaySpring Cards, Inc. Used by permission.

Chapter 7: Late Night Prayer Partner 1976 or 1977

During my years in college there were a lot of folks who gave me support and encouraged me as I prepared for the ministry with a wife who was not a Christian; there were several people who prayed regularly for Sandy and me. One story comes to mind regarding a friend named Gary Avery. Gary and I served in the Marine Corps together at South Weymouth, Massachusetts. We also attended church together in Quincy, Massachusetts. I was discharged from the Marines first and then began attending Southeastern about a year later. This story happened while we were both attending Southeastern.

I was really bothered one night about Sandy not being a Christian. I couldn't sleep, so I got up to pray for her and for us. I spent most of the next hour walking back and forth in our 12'x54' mobile home as I prayed. I mentioned this to Gary the next day at school. He told me he had also been bothered the night before, so he got up to pray for us; he had also prayed for almost an hour. When I asked him what time he was praying, it was almost the exact same time I had been praying—there was only a 15-minute difference.

It was very encouraging to know that God was in control and was raising up people to pray for us.

(2024 update: I am still in contact with Gary. He and his wife, Gina, who is now with the Lord, have been faithful supporters of whatever ministry I've been involved with for almost 50 years now.)

Gary And I
Orlando, FL
March 1997

Chapter 8: Food For The Needy March 1977

One of our closest and dearest friends while I was in college was Mrs. Virginia Chadwick, a retired professor at Southeastern and the widow of an Assemblies of God minister. She was a wonderful lady who lived about a half a mile from us. Since she didn't drive, I took Mrs. Chadwick to church with me each Sunday morning, Sunday evening and Wednesday evening. She was Casey's babysitter on a regular basis and fell in love with him.

While in college, I went to school full-time and worked part-time peddling the *Tampa Tribune* newspaper as a door-to-door solicitor. Sandy worked at the Bartow General Hospital in Bartow, Florida. We didn't have much money at all and some of what little we did have went toward Sandy's cigarettes. This was while we were living below the poverty level for five straight years.

We ate a lot of macaroni and cheese because a 19-cent box would feed the three of us for a meal. There were a few times when we ate toast three meals a day for a few days. We even experimented with it in various ways to change the taste. This is how I learned that I'm not a fan of toast with mustard and sprinkles on it.

I got up on a Sunday morning and all we had to eat for the three of us was two hot dogs and three buns. "It just so happened" (God's other name) that that was the day Mrs. Chadwick invited us over for lunch after church. I had not mentioned anything to her about our food situation. So, after church I picked Sandy up at home, told her of the invitation and we headed to Mrs. Chadwick's.

Here is what I wrote about it on March 27, 1977, in my journal: "All we had in the trailer to eat when we got up today was two dogs for the three of us. After church Mrs. Chadwick said that she'd like Sandy and I to eat with them. She didn't have to ask us twice. Praise God – He knew all we had was two hot dogs. There was a mix up in my check and I didn't get paid yet. I hadn't even prayed or thought much about it. I just figured we'd get money and buy food tomorrow. Instead of eating two hot dogs between the three of us, we each had a couple pieces of roast beef and salad and the whole works. Praise God!"

Casey And Mrs. Chadwick
Lakeland, FL
1977

Chapter 9: The Best Realtor Ever 1977-1978

One of my best friends in college was Henry Higginbotham. I got a call from him about a year or so after I graduated and had moved back to Pennsylvania. He was having trouble selling his house in Davenport, Florida; he tried for quite a while but had no serious buyers at all. Henry said he had gone to the altar at his church several times to pray about selling the house and each time it seemed as though the Lord was impressing upon him to have me advertise the house in Pennsylvania. Figuring it was his imagination, he dismissed the thought each time.

Finally, after being unable to sell the house for a period of time, he gave me a call and we talked about what he wanted me to do. Henry then gave me all the details of the house, as well as sent me some pictures. I don't remember exactly which newspapers I put the "House for Sale" ad in, but I do remember that I put it in the *Ellwood City Ledger.* I had several calls the first and only week the ad ran. One gentleman read the ad Monday night, called me Tuesday, talked to me and looked at the pictures

Wednesday, flew to Florida Thursday, and told Henry he'd buy the house Friday.

This particular story came to mind both when we were trying to sell our house in Georgia and our house in Colorado. It was so encouraging to know that God is in charge and does indeed meet our needs—even in the area of real estate.

Henry Higginbotham And Me
Pensacola, FL
1979

Chapter 10: A Step Of Faith Spring/Summer 1981

How I came into the Army as a chaplain also shows God's hand in directing our lives.

I was attending seminary at the Anderson School of Theology in Anderson, Ind., when the Lord began speaking to me about becoming a chaplain. For a period of time, I spent noon every Wednesday in the library fasting and praying for the Lord's guidance in our lives. I felt like I was between a rock and a hard place and really needed the Lord to somehow intervene. Looking at our situation from a purely human viewpoint, there aren't civilian churches that want a pastor who has a non-Christian wife.

One morning, while praying as I sat on a heater vent in our trailer, the thought came to me that I could maybe go into the military as a chaplain. My first conversation was with Sandy, who seemed to accept it as a possible area of ministry for me. After months of talking to people and checking it out, I was eventually commissioned in the Air Force Reserve as a chaplain candidate. I attended a short two-week course at Maxwell Air Force Base in Montgomery, Ala. This was followed by six weeks at Wright Patterson Air Force Base near Dayton, Ohio.

As I entered the last semester of seminary and began checking out the possibility of going into the Air Force as an active-duty chaplain, I was told I was the "wrong sex and the wrong color." At that time, the various denominations had quotas for the different branches of the service and the Church of God was "over quota" in the Air Force. Since there was a gal a year behind me in seminary planning to become an Air Force chaplain who would immediately go on active duty, the Church of God would then be even more over quota. I was told, however, that I could get into the Army after graduating from seminary.

We hadn't thought much about the Army. So, Sandy and I went to Fort Benjamin Harrison in Indianapolis, Ind., and talked to a chaplain there about the Army. We decided to go to the Army.

One of the concerns we had was that I had never been ordained. That, of course, is one of the requirements to become a chaplain. Not only had I not been ordained, but I had never even been licensed or even worked in a Church of God church in a formal, recognized way that could help in working toward ordination.

Here is where God's hand was clearly seen again. The normal procedure in the Church of God is that the individual is licensed and works in a local church for a couple of years before ordination. There is also at least one appearance before the Credentials Committee to answer questions, discuss theology, etc. None of that had occurred in my case.

So, with a letter of recommendation from the Church of God endorsing agent (and maybe another one) to the Credentials Committee of the Church of God in Western Pennsylvania, I received a letter back stating that it would be happy to ordain me for ministry in the Army. The committee just needed to know where and when. It also assured me that someone from the committee would be there to do the ordination service.

So, I had never been licensed by the Church of God, had never worked under the supervision of a Church of God pastor and had never gone before a Credentials Committee for an examination, yet I was ordained on March 15, 1981, and began active duty as a chaplain on June 13, 1981.

My final classes in seminary were the end of April 1981. I was supposed to report to Fort Monmouth, N.J., on June 14. I was concerned because I couldn't get anything in writing from the Chief of Chaplains Office. All I got were verbal promises from his staff on the phone. Now, I knew enough about the military to know that I didn't want to believe anything until it had either happened already or I had it in writing—but I couldn't get anything in writing.

We were exceptionally concerned about this since I had a job as a shift manager at a McDonalds in Anderson, we had a trailer we needed to do something with, and we needed to move Sandy and Casey back to Beaver Falls, Pennsylvania, while I was in the Officer Basic Course. The question in my mind was, "What happens if I quit my job, sell my trailer, move my family and then things fall through with the Army?"

I remember walking and praying one evening at a small park that was over the hill from where we lived in Anderson. While on the walk, I really became convinced that the Lord was indeed leading me into the Army chaplaincy and that it was time to step out on faith. So, in faith, we sold the trailer, rented a U-Haul and moved to Beaver Falls. I was supposed to leave from there on June 13 to ensure I would be at Fort Monmouth on June 14. My orders came in the mail on June 12—one day before I left for the Basic Course.

An interesting sideline to this story is that one of the papers that arrived in the mail that day was my Oath of Office to be commissioned as an officer to come on active duty. We had all kinds of trouble finding someone in the Ellwood City/Beaver Falls area who was authorized to administer the oath. We called the courthouse and a justice of the peace tried to find someone who could do it. Finally, we found a man who was a captain in the Army Reserves.

He worked at Andrews Lumber Yard on Route 65 in Ellwood City. I went to the lumber yard and asked him if he would commission me. We walked to the back of the lumber yard, I put my baseball cap on a table saw and he gave me the Oath of Office amidst the saws, lumber, sawdust and everything else.

United States Air Force
Chaplain Candidate, June 1980

Ordination Service
Ellwood City, PA
March 15, 1981

Chapter 11: A Testimony From Sandy Spring 1986

What is written below is a testimony from Sandy. I am cutting and pasting it from an email she sent Chaplain Ted Nichols a few days after he was passed over for promotion to colonel. She doesn't know that I'm putting it in here. So, in her own words from an email dated Feb. 23, 2002:

Ted,

Below you will find an epic-length (I am afraid) testimonial from me to you. It is long overdue, but maybe God has waited until "such a time as this" to prompt me to actually write it and put it into words.

Many years ago, before you even knew me, the Lord, Satan and I had a many-year struggle for my soul. I was "winning" for many years thanks, in part, to an unbelievable stubbornness to not give in to anybody who wanted to tell me what to do! Thank God, in 1982, just a month before Kelly was born, He broke me into acceptance and submission.

That was about two years before we came to Hawaii. In those two years, I pretty much kept my salvation to myself and it really didn't do much to impact my life. Things pretty much for me went along as before. Then we PCSed* to Hawaii, and I started to open up more to the Lord. I really found great joy in my first year there and became good friends with Debbi Schellhaas (now Cain). Through her, I started to attend ladies' Bible studies and enjoy Christian Women's fellowship.

After our first year there, Debbi left and we transferred up to Kolekole Chapel. Wasn't that a wonderful time to share? So many happy, fun memories. But I was not where I needed to be yet. You see, I still had to face my biggest and hardest struggle—and that was my smoking. I come from a family of very strong, orally fixated, highly strung people. Even the thought of stopping smoking made me sweat. I remember you once told Barry Davis not to quit smoking because he kind of needed it to stay calm. I was right behind him! I *needed* to smoke! Hang on, here's where you come in.

One day you were preaching at the chapel—probably from Ephesians as always :)—and you had us turn to a verse in Proverbs. Rich had bought me a brand-new Bible, and I was just beginning to write in it and mark it up for my own learning. (You should see it today. Looks like a road map from an old Johnny Carson skit of the Santa Monica freeway).

It is found on Page 985 of the NIV study Bible, if you want to turn to it. Highlighted in yellow is Proverbs 28:13, “He who conceals his sins does not prosper, but whoever confesses and renounces them finds mercy.”

It went straight to me and hit me in the heart. Right beside it, I later wrote, “To stop smoking.” It was the conviction I needed that started me on the process to stopping to smoke. I did not actually stop smoking until April of 1986, but that day started the process. And the smoking was the one and only thing that was holding me back from growth and service to the Lord. I must add something here: Also written beside that verse now in my Bible are the words “Spiritual Marker #1 Ted Nichols, Kolekole Chapel.”

That was the big start for me. Almost even bigger than the day I said “Yes” to the Lord, because that was the day I was ready to surrender my life to Him forever. You would really have to know how big a part of my life the smoking was and how it affected my walk. I actually quit smoking one day after our Kolekole ladies’ Bible study and asking those ladies to pray me through it. I was very emotional that day and convicted and totally ready to surrender. I remember Kathy Jansek crying from the emotion I felt at that moment of confession. I then ceremonially walked down to our dumpster and threw away my last cigarettes and Bic lighter. I have not had a cigarette since. And now for the “mercy” part of that verse.

That was now 16 years ago. I am not “there,” mind you, but over these years I have grown and grown and grown in my walk and knowledge of

Christ. That would have never happened as long as I smoked. I could not attend conferences or retreats, etc., because the sessions were too long for me to go without a cigarette. One of my biggest joys immediately after that day was going to the Big Island, and Rich and I roomed with the Grubbs family for what I believe was a chapel retreat. It would have never happened had I not quit smoking.

Although you and Rich have seen each other occasionally over the years, I have seen you rarely and only for short periods. I think you would be excited to see the work that the Lord has done in my life. I have learned so much about Scripture and I think I have become a pretty good mentor to some younger wives over the years. I love to study and go to church (as long as the Steelers aren't on TV). Anyway, this may be going on here too long, so I will try to close it.

There is one other thing in my Bible these days on Page 985. It is a hand-written note from Debbi Schellhaas Cain dated April 29, 1986. They had moved on by then, and I had written to her to tell her my (the Lord's) great achievement in quitting smoking. She wrote me back a wonderful note and was *so very* excited about my news. Seems she had been praying for me for $1^{1/2}$ years, without my knowledge, specifically that I would quit smoking. She and I had never even spoken about it. She said it was a testimony for me to share over and over again. It is a shame that it has taken me so long to share it with you. It also tells me that God only requires for us to do our part; we are not responsible for the results or even the whole picture. You were preaching Truth, Debbi was praying for a friend and Rich was loving me all along and never once condemned me for the smoking that I know impacted his life back then too.

I am sure that your "non-select" is the reason you and Karen have been on my mind so much lately, and Rich and I have "knocked off the grieving for us" as you asked, but I know that Satan often uses our "down" times to tell us lies. I wanted you to know a very true story and to give you a long overdue thank you for being willing to be used by God to make such significant changes for His kingdom—that is *all* that really matters at the end of the day.

Rich says I always write too many details in things. I think that is a "ladies" thing. Hope you haven't minded the long read. God bless you and continue to use you in His work. Amen.

Sandy Young

Note from Rich: I was in Korea on a month-long Team Spirit exercise when Sandy quit smoking. An interesting thing happened then: I had not prayed about her smoking. I felt pretty comfortable that the Lord would speak to her about it in His time. Well, on this particular exercise I did pray for her to quit smoking. I just remember feeling it was something I probably ought to do.

She didn't write to me while I was gone to tell me she'd quit smoking. I found out about it when I returned home. I told her that while her smoking wasn't something I normally prayed about, I had prayed for her about it while I was gone.

*PCS is the military acronym for Permanent Change of Station. It means that a servicemember and his/her family moves to a new duty assignment.

Chapter 12: God's Promise At Jump School June 1986

For some reason, one of the things I wanted to do when I was a young chaplain was to go to Airborne School and learn to parachute. It was a three-week school at Fort Benning, Georgia. We were stationed at Schofield Barracks, Hawaii, in 1986 when I finally got to go.

Airborne School was a difficult three-week school. The first week is called Ground Week; you learn to do a Parachute Landing Fall (PLF). In other words, how to land without getting hurt—at least theoretically. Learning how to do a good PLF requires throwing yourself onto the ground from different heights countless times a day.

The second week is to learn how to exit the aircraft correctly and is called Tower Week. The week is spent jumping from platforms of varying heights. The third week, Jump Week, was spent actually jumping out of airplanes—KC-130s and C-141s. Added to the rigors of throwing yourself on the ground repeatedly and the demanding physical training, there was also a significant amount of harassment from the Noncommissioned

Officer (NCO) instructors. I was also 34 years old, almost twice the age of many in my class.

I was quite nervous about the whole thing. I got to Fort Benning just in time for a four-day weekend with nothing to do except think about jumping out of a perfectly good airplane and get more nervous. I spent the time reading my Bible and praying. In doing so, I sensed very strongly that the Lord was giving me Psalm 91 as a word from Him that He would protect me and take care of me during Jump School. I memorized portions of the psalm and felt God was with me and I would not be seriously hurt.

Ground and Tower weeks went well. I wasn't at the top of my class, but I had a pretty good idea what I was doing and received the instructors' "go" to proceed to Jump Week. A "no-go" would have meant the instructors didn't think I was ready to jump out of an airplane. Had that happened, I would have been re-cycled and would have joined a class behind me to improve upon my deficiencies.

I found it quite interesting that the weekend right before our first jump, I had several classmates (much younger soldiers) come to my room to ask for a Bible, a crucifix or a cross. Each one wanted to either wear the crucifix or cross around his neck with his dog tags or put the Bible in his pocket when we jumped. The reason: So that God would protect them when we jumped. A couple of them even wanted me to be on their plane to jump with them, because "having the chaplain on my plane will ensure

I don't get hurt." In reality, they were looking for a religious good luck charm to protect them, and, for the first time in my life, I was perceived as a good luck charm.

Monday was our first jump, and it went well. Tuesday, our second jump, didn't go as planned. I remember exiting the aircraft, checking my parachute to make sure it was operating properly and getting ready to land. The next thing I remember was walking around on the Drop Zone (DZ) and saying to myself, "This doesn't look like Hawaii." I thought I had done everything correctly in preparing for and executing my landing, but I had not. Although I didn't land on my head, which would have been disastrous, I did hit my head, which could still have had very serious consequences. I had been told that any landing you can walk away from is a good one, but it didn't feel that way at the time.

It took me a minute or two to realize where I was. I remembered I was in Jump School, in Georgia, but I didn't know how many times I had already jumped. Then I heard a Black Hat (NCO instructor) say over a bullhorn, "Sit down, chaplain. We'll be there in a minute." I sat down by my parachute, which was already folded. I have no recollection of folding it.

In another minute or so the Black Hats showed up in a jeep, and a few minutes later, a Medevac (Medical Evacuation) helicopter landed on the DZ to take me to the Emergency Room (ER). The medics immobilized my head and neck, put me on a backboard and told me to make sure I didn't fall asleep on the flight to the ER. I remember two things about the flight. The first was struggling to stay awake. The second was thinking, "Lord, you promised to protect me. I'm not sure what's going on right now, but I don't feel very protected."

We landed at the emergency room, and I was rushed to the front of the line. The medical staff took X-rays of my head and neck. After the doctor read them, he told me I had a concussion and he released me to go back to my unit.

I later found out that one of the grommets in my helmet that held the safety webbing in place had broken because of the impact it sustained when I hit my head. The accident happened on Tuesday. By God's grace, I was able to jump again on Wednesday, Thursday and then graduate after jumping on Friday. The next day I flew back to Hawaii and was in chapel at Kolekole Chapel on Sunday morning.

The lesson for me was that God is faithful to His promises and to His Word, regardless of what the circumstances may look like. The weekend before Jump School started, I had clearly sensed God telling me that He would protect me from serious harm. Outward circumstances (the accident itself, being dazed on the DZ, no recollection of folding my parachute, not knowing where I was and a helicopter Medevac to the ER) might suggest that God hadn't kept that promise.

But, although I had sustained a concussion, it was not as serious as it had first appeared to be. God had, indeed, kept His promise—I was not seriously hurt. Not only did He keep His promise, but, by His grace, He also allowed me to finish and graduate. He can be trusted!

My dad pinning my jump wings on me at
graduation from Jump School.
Fort Benning, GA
June 11, 1986

Chapter 13: "It Will Be War" August 1990

While there are probably many other examples I could write about that show what God did for me during my time in the deserts of Saudi Arabia and Iraq during Operations Desert Shield and Desert Storm, two immediately come to mind. The first took place before I deployed, while the second occurred in Iraq during the war itself. This is the first:

Saddam Hussein, with about 100,000 members of the Iraqi military, invaded Kuwait on Aug. 2, 1990; he easily overran the country. I was serving as the First Brigade Chaplain in the 24th Infantry Division (Mechanized) at the time. I returned home from a parish council meeting on a Monday evening; a parish council consists of the ministry leaders in the military chapel congregation. The parish council's role is to plan and coordinate activities, develop the congregational budget, and "make things happen" ministry-wise for the congregation.

Not long after getting home, I received a telephone call telling me to go to my unit because we were being called in on an Emergency

Deployment Readiness Exercise (EDRE). An EDRE is typically a training event that begins by calling soldiers at home or the barracks, telling them to go to their unit and proceed through the steps to prepare for a real-world deployment. An EDRE is usually done for training purposes. It will identify weaknesses in deployment preparation to address. Learning from these training EDREs will help ensure a real-world deployment takes place smoothly and with less problems.

Among other things, it includes ensuring a soldier's equipment is clean and functional. The EDRE also confirms all paperwork (wills, powers of attorney, finances, etc.) are up to date. We practiced EDREs occasionally. We didn't realize it at the time, but this EDRE wasn't a training exercise—it was the real thing.

We knew it had to do with Hussein's invasion of Kuwait, but we had no idea we would, before the month was out, deploy to the Persian Gulf. Rumors abounded as to whether we would go, and if we did go, we had no idea when. The initial stages of an EDRE, at least for me, consisted of attending meetings as well as planning for chaplain coverage before and during the initial stages of the deployment itself.

Sitting in my office at about 2:00 a.m., I picked up the devotional magazine, *Our Daily Bread*, to read. I do not remember the date of the devotion I read, but the first words I saw were "It will be war." I also don't remember the rest of what I read, but I vividly recall those words. I felt as if God spoke to me about what was going to happen. The context of what I was doing at the time, coupled with current events, confirmed this to me.

> I wondered, "What are the odds that the *Our Daily Bread*, a Christian devotional, that I 'just happened' to pick up and read at 2:00 in the morning, would talk about war while I was waiting to learn if we would deploy to a potential war zone?" And that is exactly what did happen. As we deployed and eventually did go to war, I had a God-given confidence and assurance that He knew the future and was with us every step of the way.

God does not do things like that for no reason. The impact was that I went into the deployment and Operations Desert Shield and Desert Storm with the confidence that God was with us, had not forgotten us, was involved in our ministry from the very beginning and was in charge of all that would happen. Though there were many unknowns in our future, never did I doubt His presence with us—nor His involvement in and blessings on what we were doing.

Kelly, Me and Casey

Sandy and I at the First Brigade Headquarters at
Fort Stewart, GA, the day I left for Saudi Arabia and
what would become Operations Desert Shield and Desert Storm.
August 26, 1990

Chapter 14: My Vehicle, An Oil Leak And Prayer February-March 1991

The second testimony from Iraq has to do with my vehicle. The official name for it was a Commercial Utility Cargo Vehicle, but we simply knew it as a CUCV. Though not an expert on cars and trucks, I considered it to be an Army-style Chevy Blazer.

Having it in good operating condition was crucial for me to do my job as a brigade chaplain. I needed the ability to get to soldiers to visit them, counsel them, and to provide worship services and Bible studies. I also needed it to visit the chaplains I supervised and to attend unit and chaplain meetings. The vehicle was critical, since the brigade was spread out across a 50-mile (85-kilometer) swath of the desert.

The ground war had begun, and after traveling hundreds of miles across the desert from Saudi Arabia into Iraq, we noticed our CUCV had an oil leak. Every day we could see more oil leaking from the vehicle and yet every morning when we checked it, the oil was full. We even took it to the mechanics, and they couldn't find the problem. They verified it had a leak, yet the oil level was always full.

No one understood how this could be until I got a letter from Sandy. In it, she said she had been praying for me, which she always did, but recently her prayers had focused on my vehicle. She knew we were on the move across the desert, and she knew my vehicle was a necessity for my ministry, so she was praying specifically for my CUCV.

Little did either of us know at the time that the Lord was answering her prayers to take care of me the same way He took care of the widow of Zarephath. Elijah told this widow to use the rest of her flour and oil to make bread for him, her son and herself. She did so, and ". . . the jar of flour was not used up and the jug of oil did not run dry, in keeping with the word of the Lord spoken by Elijah." (1 Kings 17:16)

Truly something only God could do!

Chapter 15: Change In Rating Scheme Summer 1993

A very important consideration for an Army officer in regards to promotions is which individuals write his or her annual Officer Efficiency Report (OER). I think the civilian terminology for an OER would be a performance review. The people who write the OER are those for whom the officer works. Collectively, they are referred to as the "rating scheme," because they rate the officer's performance. Although not always, these officers are usually of a higher military rank. In the account below, I was a major at the time, my immediate supervisor (called the rater) was a lieutenant colonel and my senior supervisor (called the senior rater) was a colonel.

It is the OERs that go before a promotion board to determine if you get promoted. The promotion board reviews, among other things, the OERs from all the officers considered for promotion and then selects those deemed worthy of promotion. In considering an officer for promotion, the evaluation by the senior rater carries the most weight.

I initially got along very well with my senior rater, who was the Area Support Group Commander in Hanau, Germany. He liked me so well that at least once he sent some of the things I said in one of my sermons to his subordinate commanders. He also placed me in the position of the Base Support Battalion Chaplain instead of two chaplains who were senior to me in rank. My senior rater and I got along well for the first two years.

Chaplain (Colonel) Jimmy Roberts (not his real name) came to Hanau in 1993 as the senior chaplain. I worked for him my last year there. As the senior chaplain, Chaplain Roberts had the authority to change my rating scheme; in other words, the authority to determine who rated my performance and wrote my OERs. For reasons I didn't understand completely, he changed my rating scheme so that the commander who I had gotten along with so well was no longer my senior rater—he was not even in my rating scheme at all. Chaplain Roberts made himself my senior rater.

The next year was a very difficult year for me and the chaplaincy in Hanau. There were accusations of chaplain financial mismanagement, which were later proven to be untrue. Thanks to a vengeful gossiper, there was also severe discord in the Protestant Women of the Chapel (the chapel's ladies group) that spilled over into the congregation I served.

In addition to that, Chaplain Roberts assigned a Christian Scientist chaplain, who was a higher military rank than I was, to co-pastor the Main

Post Protestant congregation with me. When I told Chaplain Roberts I could not, in good conscience, co-pastor with a Christian Scientist, he removed me from the congregation I had pastored for two years. For these reasons, especially my refusal to co-pastor with a Christian Scientist, I fell out of grace with the commander. I'd fallen out of grace so badly that I left Hanau without an award of any kind. For an Army officer who has done even a half-decent job, to leave a three-year assignment without an award of any kind, is almost unheard of.

As mentioned above, Chaplain Roberts had changed my rating scheme a year earlier so that he was my senior rater. God's hand was clearly in this change. Since the commander, my previous senior rater, refused to give me an award, there is no way he would have given me a good OER; a bad or even mediocre OER would have been difficult to overcome in getting promoted to lieutenant colonel.

Although Chaplain Roberts and I did not see eye-to-eye on several things, by God's grace, he respected me. I think this was due to my honesty and forthrightness in giving him my thoughts and opinions on different issues—even if they differed from his. He also respected the fact that I refused to compromise my convictions by agreeing to co-pastor with a Christian Scientist.

At one point, Chaplain Roberts even gave me a handwritten note thanking me for my candor when speaking to him on a particular subject. Despite our differences, he gave me a very good OER, which no doubt was instrumental in both my promotions to lieutenant colonel and later to colonel. There is no way I would have received an OER like that from my previous senior rater, but—in the providence of God—Chaplain Roberts had changed my rating scheme a year earlier.

Praise God that He is always at work, even in the difficult and confusing times.

Chapter 16: Providence Of God And Promotions 1996

Chaplain promotion boards consist of five or six officers. I think three are chaplains; the other members of the board are non-chaplain officers from across the Army. One of the non-chaplain officers on my promotion board to lieutenant colonel was Col. Bob Fletcher.

I had worked for him twice. We were in 2/7 Infantry Battalion together and in the First Brigade; he was my executive officer and my rater (immediate supervisor) both times. This means that, during my promotion board, Col. Fletcher was reading Officer Efficiency Reports in my file that he himself had written about me—which, I have to believe, greatly helped my chances of being selected for promotion.

Out of all the officers in the Army, Sandy and I don't believe it was a coincidence that Col. Fletcher was chosen to serve on the chaplain promotion board when I was being considered for promotion. It was, to us, a confirmation of God's hand in the selection process and His direction in our lives.

Promotion to lieutenant colonel. Chaplain (Colonel) Don Hanchett and Sandy. Oct 1, 1996

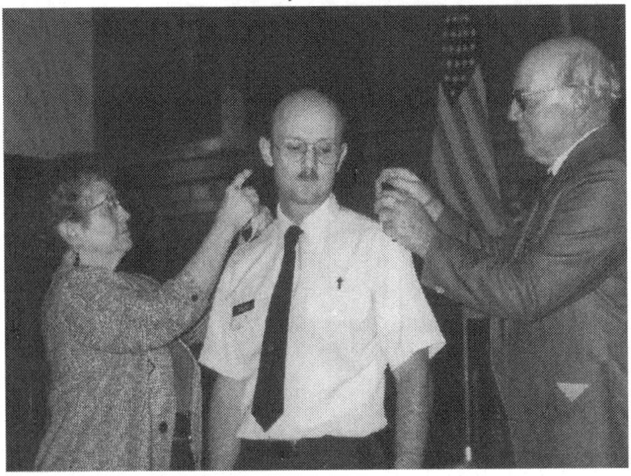

Promotion to lieutenant colonel. Mom and Dad putting my chevrons on.

Chapter 17: Housing At Fort Bliss May 1996

Being selected for promotion to lieutenant colonel necessitated a move from Fort Carson, Colo., to Fort Bliss, in El Paso, Texas. Because we enjoyed Colorado so much, and found the ministry at Fort Carson to be meaningful and rewarding, I went to my installation chaplain (the senior chaplain on an Army post) and asked if there were any plans in the works for me to be re-assigned to another installation.

Since chaplain assignments were set by the Chief of Chaplains' Office (a chaplain with the rank of major general and the senior chaplain in the Army) in the Pentagon, my installation chaplain called to ask if I would be leaving Fort Carson. After talking to him, my installation chaplain assured me that there were no plans to re-assign me. But for reasons that were never made known to me, that decision quickly changed. Six days later, I was not only told I would be leaving Fort Carson, but I had my orders in hand for Fort Bliss.

There are many things for a family to consider when moving from one assignment to another. Where you will live is at the top of the list. There seem to be countless things to consider when deciding where you'll call home.

Where you live determines where the kids go to school, how far the daily commute is and whether you can get by with one car or if you'll need two. If there is no availability for military housing on post, you want to know how long the waiting list is; waiting to move to housing on post necessitates moving twice—once to a rental property, then moving onto post once housing becomes available. If you don't want to be on the waiting list, then you must decide if you want to rent or buy. These are just a few of the seemingly endless decisions you need to make.

With these things on our minds, Sandy and I drove from Colorado Springs to Fort Bliss for a few days to investigate the housing and schooling situations. When we arrived, I spoke to the Housing Office—the office responsible for monitoring housing vacancies and assigning housing to incoming soldiers. I was told that it would be several months, possibly a year, before a housing unit would become available for us.

Needing a place to live, we went apartment hunting since we wanted to live on post rather than rent or buy a house. After looking around, we found an apartment complex and signed the paperwork to lease the apartment in about a month. The apartment manager understood that we were waiting for post housing; he assured us we would be able to move out when housing became available and that there would be no penalty for breaking the lease.

With that information, we headed back to Colorado Springs the next day. Our stop for the first night was in Santa Fe, N.M. While in our motel late that afternoon, I received a call from the Fort Bliss Housing Office telling me that housing would be available for us when we arrived a month later. I do not know the details as to why or how things changed. I do know, however, that we went from a year's waitlist to having it available when we arrived. God orders our steps in definite ways—and takes care of the details. To God be the glory!

A rare snow at Fort Bliss, in El Paso, Texas.

Chapter 18: Still The Best Realtor Ever June 1996

By the time I retired from the Army, Sandy and I had moved 17 times since getting married. Other than Hawaii, the place we enjoyed the most was Colorado Springs. We liked our house, the schools, the area, the post, the job, the chapel—we liked everything about our assignment. While there, I came out on the promotion list for lieutenant colonel, which often means being re-assigned to another Army post. I was assured, however, that I wouldn't be. Despite that assurance, I was re-assigned, and it was the quickest I'd ever received re-assignment orders. They arrived in less than a week, and we had our house on the real estate market a week after that.

Selling a house isn't any fun. Real estate agents can bring potential buyers by to look at the listing at just about any time. Every showing to a prospective buyer meant we had work to do—things like vacuuming the carpet, wiping the counters, and ensuring that nothing was lying around and everything was in its proper place. We then needed to leave the house while it was being shown. Casey worked at McDonalds for the summer, and we went there so many times that they began to give us free food.

The house finally did sell—on the 54th showing. That is where God comes in. When the house finally sold, it was shown by a real estate company called Faith Realty; it was an agency owned by Christians and the house was sold to Christians. While other real estate agencies showed our house more than once, it was the first and only time Faith Realty showed the house that it sold. We had been praying to sell the house, and the couple that bought it had been praying for the right house for them. God answered both our prayers on the 54th showing through a Christian real estate agency.

God still is the best realtor ever!

Chapter 19: Angels On Interstate 25 June 1996

We had been stationed at Fort Carson in Colorado Springs, Colo., for two years when it was time to move to Fort Bliss in El Paso, Texas. Since it was about a 600-mile trip, we decided to drive both cars to Fort Bliss. Kelly and I were going in our Pontiac LeMans; Sandy and Casey would follow a week later in our Plymouth Voyager.

Kelly and I began our trip. We drove a couple of hours south on I-95 and stopped at a rest area. When we did, I noticed smoke seeping out around the hood. I am certainly no mechanic, but after popping the hood, I could see my radiator and hoses were all OK. Next, I checked the oil. It was leaking and was low. I put some oil in it and we drove to Trinidad, Colo., where I found a mechanic to look at it.

We ended up leaving it in a garage overnight while Kelly and I stayed in a hotel (and watched the Brady Bunch Movie). The car was packed full, including our computer—since we were in the middle of moving from Colorado to Texas. Leaving our car, with our computer, along with everything else we packed, in a strange garage in a strange city wasn't a good feeling. The garage mechanic checked the car and said one of the bolts that held my oil pan on was stripped. He said it needed to be tapped out so the bolt would fit better, but he had fixed it the best he could. He thought we'd be OK to continue traveling. Hoping and praying our car would make it, we headed off across the New Mexico desert for El Paso.

I don't remember much about what happened the next day except that we spent the next night in Albuquerque where I had the car checked out at another garage. The mechanic tightened the bolt the best he could, and we headed across the desert again. Nearing the Texas border, the car started losing power. At one point, I pulled off the road and coasted to a stop along I-25 when the car began running OK again, so I continued to drive.

I was nearing an exit when the car began giving me trouble yet again. As I pulled off the exit, the car konked out and I began coasting—right into a General Motors dealer on the left side of the road in Anthony, Texas. If the GM dealer had been another couple hundred yards farther, we would have had to push the car. But it wasn't, and I coasted right into the parking lot.

The issue with the car this time was unrelated to the first problem. A mechanic got the car running so we could get the rest of the way to Fort Bliss. I'm not sure if there really were angels on I-25 that day, but there is no doubt that God was with us. He not only provided a GM dealer for us right when we needed one, but He also took us straight to it.

Chapter 20: Division Chaplain 1998-1999

This next story, which has to do with how I became the division chaplain of the 25th Infantry Division (Light) at Schofield Barracks, Hawaii, is complex. There is no doubt, however, that God's hand was in it.

To set the stage, an Army division is a fighting unit commanded by a major general (MG). The 25th Infantry Division (Light) had roughly 10,000 soldiers in it. The division chaplain is the senior chaplain in the division and who is responsible for all the religious support (ministry) to the soldiers and their families within the division. Of course, no one chaplain can meet all the religious needs of that many people; in my case, I think I had 23 subordinate chaplains, who, along with their chaplain assistants (enlisted soldiers who help the chaplain), carried out the ministry in their units.

Only a small percentage of chaplains ever become a division chaplain. An individual must first be selected for lieutenant colonel (LTC). Then they must be selected to attend the Division Chaplain Course at the

United States Army Chaplain Center and School, where they are taught how to be a division chaplain. Both the selection to LTC and to the Division Chaplain Course are a competitive selection process based on Officer Efficiency Reports (OERs).

After being selected for LTC and attending the Division Chaplain Course, the chaplain then waits to see if the Chief of Chaplains (the senior chaplain in the Army, a major general) nominates him or her to a division commander to be their division chaplain. It is a privilege to be nominated, and all you can do is feel extremely blessed and thankful if you are.

I was in my office one day at Fort Bliss when I was told I had received a call from a MG Hill, who wanted me to call him. I had worked for MG Hill about fifteen years earlier when he was a LTC and was the battalion commander for the 1/35 Infantry Battalion; I was a captain at the time. It was anticipated that MG Hill would go to Hawaii and become the commanding general of the 25th Infantry Division (Light) at Schofield Barracks.

I didn't know it, but MG Hill was on temporary duty to Fort Bliss. He saw my name on the front of our house while he was running one morning and had his secretary track me down to come and see him. I did so, and we had a nice visit for about a half an hour, during which we discussed me potentially coming to work for him as his division chaplain. I then went back to my office where the senior chaplain on post (my boss) told me that I needed to get on MG Hill's calendar again so I could let him know that the way chaplain assignments frequently worked was that if he would call the Chief of Chaplains and request that I become his division chaplain, then the Chief of Chaplains would likely grant his request.

This was a possibility since I had already been selected for LTC and had been to the Division Chaplain Course. I thought about talking to MG Hill again, but thought this would be playing politics, and I did not want to do that. I decided that if I talked to anyone, it would be the Lord. Feeling that the Lord could make me a division chaplain if He wanted me to be one, I trusted Him to do so and did not reach out to MG Hill.

As anticipated, MG Hill did go to Hawaii to command the 25th Infantry Division (Light). About that same time, I was told I was going to leave Fort Bliss, but I didn't know yet where I would go next. At one point, I was supposed to go to the Army Material Command in Alexandria, Virginia. I was also told I might go to Atlanta to work for Forces Command (FORSCOM); an assignment to Bad Kreuznach, Germany, was also a possibility. I don't know the details of what happened, but I was finally told that I would be going to Fort Shafter, Hawaii—about 25 miles from where MG Hill was commanding the 25th Infantry Division (Light).

Totally unbeknownst to me, the chaplain I would replace at Fort Shafter and the current division chaplain had heard of me because MG Hill had mentioned my name in a speech he had given to chaplains.

When these chaplains both heard I was coming to Hawaii, they told MG Hill that he could call the Chief of Chaplains to request that I become his next division chaplain when the current one went to another assignment. Providentially, they told him the exact same thing that the senior chaplain at Fort Bliss wanted me to tell him a year earlier. MG Hill did call the Chief of Chaplains and asked him to assign me as the division chaplain for the 25th Infantry Division (Light). The Chief of Chaplains did so, and I became the division chaplain on June 14, 1999.

To confirm that God's hand was involved in my becoming a division chaplain necessitates another story. The senior chaplain at Fort Bliss (and my boss) saw it as his responsibility to be an advocate for his subordinate chaplains in helping them achieve their military career goals. He talked to me one on one to find out what I wanted to do in the future. He asked if I wanted to be a division chaplain. I said I wouldn't turn down the opportunity to be a division chaplain, but that I would be just as happy to be given a congregation to pastor on an Army base somewhere.

Sandy and I went to the 25th feeling confident that the Lord had sent us there. We have never politicked for a job or a promotion, and we didn't then either. Nor did we request that a senior chaplain advocate on our behalf. We are very thankful God opened the doors to be the division chaplain for the 25th Infantry Division (Light), the Tropic Lightning Division. It was the highlight of my military ministry as well as humbling to know that both the Army and the Lord trusted me with that responsibility. More importantly, however, was the point that we had done our best to put Him first, and He took care of the rest.

Change Of Stole Ceremony
Soldier's Chapel
Schofield Barracks, HI
June 14, 1999

Sandy and I after the Change of Stole Ceremony when I assumed the responsibilities of the division chaplain of the
25th Infantry Division (Light).
Schofield Barracks, HI
June 14, 1999

Chapter 21: Changing Denominations 2000

After spending a significant amount of time studying, thinking and praying, I decided to test the waters to see if I should transfer my ordination from the Church of God (Anderson, Ind.) to the Presbyterian Church in America (PCA). I asked a friend and PCA chaplain, Jim Carter, to get me in touch with Dave Peterson, the PCA endorser. I wanted to learn what the procedure was and how difficult it might be to transfer my ordination and endorsement to the PCA.

An endorser, or endorsing agent, is a key person for chaplains; the endorser is the intermediary between the prospective chaplain and the military. It is the endorser who provides an ecclesiastical endorsement for a chaplain to go on active duty. He does this by verifying the prospective chaplain is academically, experientially and spiritually qualified to serve on active duty. This includes attesting that the individual is an ordained minister who is good standing with the denomination.

My guess is that either Jim or Dave forgot about my request, because I didn't hear anything back from either. I waited a year until I followed up with Jim; this time things immediately began to fall into place.

I contacted Jim in either November or December of 1999. It "just so happened" that both Dave Peterson and I were already scheduled to be at the Chief of Chaplain Conference in January of 2000. Neither of us knew the other would be there. Stan Beach, a retired Navy chaplain who worked for Dave, also "just so happened" to be scheduled to be in Hawaii about a week after the Chief's conference. I was able to meet with both of them, get guidance from them and begin the process. I sensed that the Lord was pulling things together, and that I needed to pursue the transfer.

I spent much of the next nine or 10 months studying for my oral exam before the Northern California Presbytery. A Presbytery is a body of church elders who, among other responsibilities, have the task of examining those desiring ordination, to ensure they are theologically sound. Questions cover a range of topics such as Bible knowledge, theology, doctrine and personal experience, among other things. Most of the churches in the Northern California Presbytery were, of course, located in northern California; there were just two or three churches in Hawaii. That being the case, most of the quarterly Presbytery meetings were in California. Even so, it "just so happened" that the next Presbytery meeting was going to be in Hawaii, which is where I was. Expensive travel to California would not be necessary. This was another confirmation that I should pursue the transfer.

Being a division chaplain and pastor of the main post Protestant congregation, plus studying for the Presbytery exam, kept me burning the midnight oil. I was feeling overwhelmed and discouraged one week in particular and was really wondering whether or not it was worth all the work. I was about ready to throw in the towel and forget about transferring my ordination when I got an unsolicited email from Stan Beach. He asked when the Presbytery was meeting and said he might just show up. That was the encouragement I needed at the exact time I needed it.

The time came for the Presbytery exam and it went pretty well—until I was asked to discuss my theology of the Baptism in the Holy Spirit. I froze on the question and drew a blank. Because of my Pentecostal background, I was concerned I might get some trick questions and thought this might be one of them. Although this was not a trick question, I couldn't come up with an answer. After the Presbyters asked all their questions, I left the room for them to decide my fate.

Unbeknownst to me, they were very concerned about my inability to answer the Baptism in the Holy Spirit question and they didn't know what to do because I had done fine otherwise. Bill Manning, a chaplain friend who was ordained by the PCA, came out and talked to me in the hallway while they were discussing what they should do procedurally. We talked about the Holy Spirit and Bill helped me put my thoughts together on the subject. (The ironic thing is that I had secretly hoped Bill wouldn't attend the Presbytery meeting: I thought I would feel better if no one I knew was there, in case I made a complete fool of myself. As it turned out, Bill was the one who unknowingly pulled me through.)

Bottom line—I went back to the Credentials Committee and we talked for a few minutes. Then I went before the Presbytery again, explained my answer and was voted unanimously into the Presbytery.

I saw God's hand in the transferring of my ordination and endorsement in several different ways:

1. It just so happened that Dave Peterson and I would be at the same conference.
2. It just so happened Stan Beach was already scheduled to be in Hawaii the week after the conference.
3. It just so happened the next Presbytery meeting of the Northern California Presbytery was going to be in Hawaii.
4. It just so happened that Stan emailed me during an overwhelming and discouraging time.
5. It just happened that Bill Manning did attend the Presbytery meeting and was there to help me during my exam.

It is no wonder at all that I frequently say that God's other name is "It Just So Happened."

Chapter 22: Presidential Election Of 2000 November 2000

At the time, the election of November 2000 was like none other. Vice President Al Gore ran against the Texas governor, George W. Bush. The eight years under President Clinton and Vice President Gore had been horrendous for Christians, for morality, for the unborn, and for most things that reflect God's character and priorities.

George W. Bush, during a campaign interview, had said that Jesus Christ was the most influential person in his life. He went on to explain that Billy Graham had led him to the Lord. Christians and conservatives were excited to see someone like him running for president.

Without going into all the details about the election, the winner wasn't decided for more than a month after Election Day. There were recounts, court battles, Supreme Court rulings and other things before the winner was finally determined.

The outcome wasn't decided until around the second week of December, with George W. Bush eventually being declared the victor.

One of my scripture verses that same day in *Tabletalk**was I Samuel 15:28: "Samuel said to him [Saul], 'The Lord has torn the kingdom of Israel from you today and has given it to one of your neighbors—to one better than you.'"

I don't see that as being coincidental. Romans 13:1 reminds us, "Let every person be subject to the governing authorities. For there is no authority except from God, and those that exist have been instituted by God." God was confirming that He had rejected Al Gore and chosen someone who would seek to govern in accordance with biblical principles.

**Tabletalk* is the monthly magazine published by Ligonier Ministries.

Chapter 23: Peace Of God And An MRI April 8, 2002

I had been having some trouble with my right knee for several months. My doctor didn't know if it was arthritis or a torn meniscus. An MRI would be the answer—it would tell him what he needed to know. The MRI was scheduled for today.

Having heard stories from folks who have had MRIs, I didn't like what they had to say. To start with, I was—and still am—claustrophobic, and then hearing folks talk about not being able to move at all for as long as 45 minutes concerned me. Because of that, I went to the MRI very well prepared. I took an herbal supplement to help me relax about 30 minutes before the MRI. I also had my CD player with Ray Boltz singing contemporary Christian songs along with me. Even so, I was still a little nervous about having the procedure.

The gal running the MRI machine immobilized my knee so I couldn't move it. Next, she put me in the MRI machine tunnel, and I immediately had a couple distressing thoughts about how I couldn't move and needed to get out of there. Just then, the CD came on loud and clear, with Ray Boltz singing "The Anchor Holds."

As soon as he started singing, I calmed down 100 percent, had a tear come out of each eye and roll down my cheeks, and just felt the peace of God in an unbelievable way. I would be tempted to give the credit to the herbal supplement, except for the exact timing—the thoughts I was having that I needed to get away, the song, the tears and the peace. It had to be the Lord!

He once again showed His faithfulness in my time of need.

Chapter 24: A Change In Operating Room Plans April 21, 2002

Today is April 26, 2002. I had arthroscopic knee surgery a few days ago at Cushing Hospital, a small hospital in Leavenworth, Kan. How I ended up at Cushing is the story.

I'd been having knee problems for about eight months. The doctor, after seeing my MRI results, decided I needed to have surgery for a torn meniscus in my right knee. I was supposed to have the operation at Munson Health Care Clinic on Fort Leavenworth, since arthroscopic surgery for a torn meniscus is supposed to be relatively easy.

I began my pre-admission paperwork about two weeks before the scheduled surgery. When the nurse anesthetist learned my mom had malignant hypothermia and almost died after her mastectomy, she immediately stopped and said, "We can't do your surgery here. We'll have to go downtown." The reason was that malignant hypothermia is familial and clinic protocol required that an anesthesiologist and an intensive care unit be on site. Lacking both of these at the clinic, we went to Cushing.

The surgery itself went well. The recovery room was closed, since it was later in the day, so they used the ICU as a recovery room. It was there that I had a reaction to the anesthesia. It wasn't anything like mom had had, but I was very dizzy and my blood pressure went wacky. It was quite high initially, but then I started feeling funny in my stomach, started sweating and my blood pressure dropped quite low. And where was I when this happened? Right in the ICU with an ICU nurse.

Had the surgery not occurred at Cushing I wouldn't have been in the ICU with an ICU nurse right there to take care of me. I don't know what would have happened if I had had the reaction at Munson, but we are confident of the Lord's hand in the move to Cushing and even the ICU being used as a recovery room.

Chapter 25: Promotion To Colonel 2002

We saw God's hand in my selection for promotion to colonel in a couple of ways. For starters, I had been passed over for promotion the first year I was eligible. About 45 percent of the lieutenant colonels who were eligible for selection to colonel that year were selected.

Even though an officer, in this case a lieutenant colonel, has been passed over in a particular year, he or she is still eligible for promotion to colonel in subsequent years. Getting selected the next year—which is called being "above the zone"—does happen, but not very often, as the selection rates are usually lower than 5 percent of those being considered. This is when I was selected—in my second year of consideration.

Secondly, the promotion board results were announced on Feb. 20, 2002. Sandy's scripture for her devotions that day was Luke 12:48: "From everyone who has been given much, much will be demanded." That scripture, on that day, was a confirmation of God's hand on the results of the promotion board.

In hindsight, and after seeing what God did while I was stationed at Fort Monmouth, where I would be assigned as a colonel, there is no doubt about God's hand in my promotion.

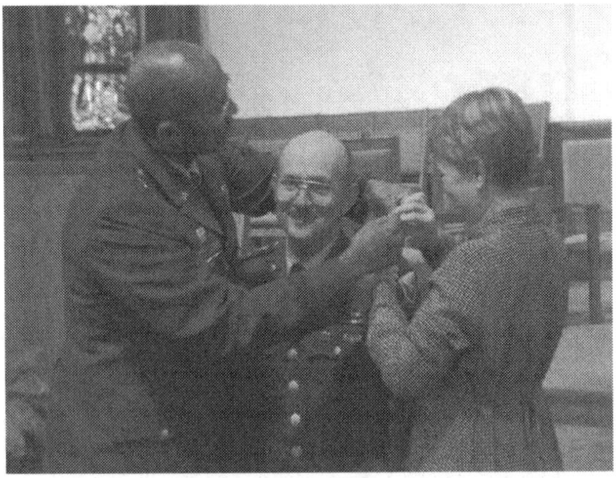

Major General Bill Russ and Sandy pinning my Eagles on when I was promoted to colonel.

Kelly (l.) and Casey (r.) were able to attend my promotion to colonel.
Main Post Chapel Fort Monmouth, NJ September 27, 2002

Chapter 26: Medical Issues Arise Fall 2002

During the latter part of 2002 I became ill and eventually required prostate surgery. The Lord's hand was so evident throughout the whole ordeal. To begin with, there was the timing of me getting sick. I was away from home on temporary duty (TDY) to Washington, D.C., two separate times in September of 2002.

I left Washington on Wednesday, September 25, to return home after the second TDY; that afternoon, Sandy and I went to Newark Airport and picked up family members who were flying in to attend my promotion ceremony. I was promoted on September 27 at 3:30 p.m. By 2:00 a.m. the next morning I was unable to urinate, had a fever and would be in the emergency room later that morning. I had been sick the day of my promotion, but had attributed it to nerves. That wasn't the case—it turned out I had an enlarged prostate and an infection.

It may seem strange to say it like this, but the timing of getting sick was wonderful. It hadn't happened a year earlier when I was gone half the time assigned to the Battle Command Training Program (BCTP). It did not even happen a few days earlier when I was in Washington.

The Lord let me do my job at BCTP, get through both Washington TDYs and even get promoted before getting sick. We're thankful for His hand in the timing of the onset of the problem.

We're also thankful for the timing of my surgery. Of course, I would have liked to have had it sooner, but November 26 was the date. To have the surgery much later than that would have made it difficult for me to be back at the chapel for Christmas services. Being recovered enough to preach the Sunday service on December 22 and to conduct the Christmas Eve Candlelight Service had been my prayer. God graciously answered this prayer and I was able to do both.

We have also seen God's hand in the many Christian friends He provided for us. I received countless cards, emails and calls from great brothers and sisters in the Lord who truly ministered to me. Their thoughts and prayers were greatly appreciated!

Chapter 27: Publicity And The Purpose Driven Life Campaign Fall 2002

While most of these *God In My Life* testimonies were written after the fact, this one was written while we were in the midst of preparing for the Purpose Driven Life campaign we conducted at our chapel in October of 2002. Here is what I wrote:

As I write this, we are still a month away from the campaign. It is exciting to even imagine what the Lord is going to do. He has been actively involved so far—even in our publicity.

The first area is that of a banner across the Avenue of Memories, the main street after driving through the front gate of the fort. I requested to have a banner made and then hung over the street for a month. I received a call from the sign office saying the Equal Opportunity office (EO) already had the location booked for a couple of months this fall.

I talked to the gentleman a few minutes about it and very kindly explained that we had been turned down for a banner for the National Prayer Breakfast last year and, since the EO office had so many month-long programs, it seemed as though it had a monopoly on the location. We discussed my options, and I told him I would call him back regarding what I wanted to do. The very next day, he called me and said they had decided to "bump" the EO banner and would do all I had requested. He also volunteered to make a smaller banner and to place it at a different gate so people coming into Fort Monmouth via that gate would also see it.

Also, a week later I got a call from the woman who sends out the retiree newsletter to several thousand local military retirees. She said, "Chaplain Young, I'm not sure what the 'Purpose' stuff is, but I'd be glad to publicize it for you in my next newsletter. I can give you a short narrative or a full-page ad. Just let me know." This was unsolicited help.

Then, just this week I opened a big envelope delivered to the chapel. It contained addresses for all the people recently assigned to government housing on Fort Monmouth. This will provide us with many new leads and was also more unsolicited help. I have no idea where they came from or who initiated it, but praise God it made it to my desk.

Chapter 28: Purpose Driven Life Campaign October 2002

There is no way to adequately explain all that God did during our campaign, and this short testimony will not do it justice. While Sunday morning worship attendance didn't increase that much, other areas have seen significant growth. Three years ago, we had about 15 people attend our Tuesday night Bible study. Two years ago, we had 35. Now we're averaging close to 120 when you consider youth and children.

We have used every available space and the next place to host a Bible study would have been my office. Many people, including several Catholics, have a new hunger for God's Word. We now have a Kids of the Chapel program and an exceptionally good youth group. Our music program has finally come together. Many people who used to be spectators in the chapel are now active participants who are seeking God, following Him and getting involved in chapel life. Only eternity will show us all that God has done during this time. Praise Him!

Chapter 29:
Notifying Next Of Kin
July 8, 2003

Continuing for several years, Operation Iraqi Freedom was an armed conflict spearheaded by the United States. It led to both the capture of Saddam Hussein, Iraq's dictator, and the defeat of the Iraqi forces. Part of my ministry included going with another officer to a family's home to tell them when their loved one had been killed. God's hand was very apparent as we made one of these notifications in Hillside, N.J.—a city adjacent to Newark.

The other officer, Maj. John Macey, and I left Fort Monmouth, in central Jersey, at about 6:10 p.m. and headed for Hillside. We got off the New Jersey Turnpike and within minutes were very lost and had no idea where to go. We had three different maps and, other than the main road, we couldn't find a single street that was on any of our maps.

We wandered around for about thirty minutes trying to find our way. Eventually, we stopped at a gas station to ask for directions, but the attendant was unable to help. Then we called back the Fort Dix Casualty

Office (the office responsible for notifying families and helping them through the difficult times ahead) hoping they could do a computer search to help us find the address. They couldn't!

We continued to drive around looking. Finally, Maj. Macey pulled off the side of the road and called his wife to see if she could help via the computer. We pulled away from the curb after talking to her, saw a street sign and realized we were about three blocks from where we wanted to be. Given the size of the Newark area, this was unbelievable and an answer to prayer. We went into the house, broke the sad news to the family, stayed a little while and came back to Fort Monmouth, arriving there about 9:30 or 9:45 p.m.

I went to work the next morning and was talking to Jim Kelly, our Catholic parish coordinator and an ordained Catholic deacon. He said he had been unable to get me off his mind the evening before and had prayed for me throughout the evening. He began praying at 6:00 p.m. and said his last prayer about 10:00 p.m.—almost the exact time we were traveling, getting lost, delivering the sad news and returning home. We were both kind of awestruck when we realized the timing of his prayers and our need for them. Praise God!

And, to top things off, after we spent the evening together making this notification, Maj. Macey and his family began attending chapel.

Chapter 30:
God Provides, God Confirms
Summer 2003

It was the middle of the summer, and I'd been in awe of all the Lord's recent answers to prayer. Certainly, the next-of-kin notification just shared was one of them. But there were many other examples of God answering prayers in ways that just "had" to be Him getting involved in our lives.

The summer started with Chaplain Randy Walker, the Fort Monmouth Garrison Chaplain, leaving for Fort Sill, Okla. He left about the third week of June; Randy's replacement, Chaplain Jack Woodford, wasn't scheduled to arrive at Fort Monmouth and be ready for work until the first or second week of September. That means I was going to be by myself most of the summer. By God's grace, things went very smoothly with no major crisis as I tried to keep all the balls in the air.

A couple of great unexpected helps were two Reserve chaplains—one Air Force and one Army. The Air Force chaplain did a graveside service for me and would be available for other things as they came along. The Army chaplain conducted a funeral for me in Jersey City, which is where he lived and pastored. The wars in Afghanistan and Iraq were adding to my workload, as I needed to notify next of kin and conduct any subsequent follow-up. I praise God that He sent in extra help to lessen the load.

Earlier in the year, we began laying the groundwork for a "40 Days of Purpose" campaign in the fall. Part of that groundwork was trusting the Lord to have more people participate in the campaign than we could drum up ourselves. The number I was initially hoping for was 250 participants.

I asked the leaders of the congregation to come to a meeting to tell them about the campaign. My role in the meeting was to provide them with my vision for the congregation regarding the campaign. As I prayed that Tuesday morning, the thought came to mind that 250 people wasn't enough and that I should trust the Lord for 500. My initial response was, "Yeah, right."

I didn't think of the thought as being from the Lord. As I considered it throughout the day, however, I became pretty convinced that the number should be 500. As I pondered it that afternoon, I said a prayer that went something like this, "Lord, I'm getting ready to make a fool of myself tonight by announcing that we are preparing for 500 people to attend and getting ready to spend another $3,500 that will be wasted if I'm wrong. Will you please confirm the number 500 to me?"

I then left the chapel and headed for my car. I immediately ran into Shirley Simmons, one of our congregants who would oversee executing our plans. As we talked, I told her I didn't think 250 was enough to trust the Lord for. She said she didn't think so either. I then asked her what she thought was a good number. Her response, "Five hundred." God answered my prayer and gave me confirmation of the 500 less than five minutes after I had asked him for it.

Chapter 31: The Kids Move Away Summer 2003

At the time I originally wrote this, the previous couple of weeks had been difficult for Sandy and me—especially Sandy. We had been spoiled the last year by only being 400 miles from our son Casey and his family, and we'd had the opportunity to see them halfway regularly. Plus, Kelly was in college just a few miles from Casey, so we got a "two-fer" out of each visit—we got to see both our kids.

I had allowed myself to get too excited at times about retiring near my kids and being an "up-close-and-personal" grandpa. However, all that changed when Casey and his family moved to Minnesota. I had no plans to retire near Minnesota. I was happy for them and am confident the Lord was the one who opened the door for them—but it was still awfully hard to tell them good-bye though, which we did on a Monday night.

Something happened as we pulled away that is really difficult to describe—yet it was most definitely the Lord. Sandy was crying hard, and I was beginning to sob. Suddenly, I immediately quit crying as quickly as if someone had turned off a faucet; it happened just that quickly. Then four words came to my mind—"He's in My will."

I wasn't then, and still am not, a huge fan of sentences beginning with the words, "God spoke to me," because I've heard some pretty off-the-wall things following those words. That said, I do believe it was the Lord. I can honestly say that Casey moving to Minnesota hasn't bothered me since then. I am genuinely happy for them and excited about the new possibilities the Lord has for them in their future.

Praise God—He has our kids in His Hands too!

Chapter 32: Retirement Or One More Assignment? Spring/Summer 2005

I write today on April 18, 2005, wondering where the Lord will lead us after the Army. Our current plans are to put in retirement papers for Aug. 1, 2006. A couple of interesting things have happened so far:

I spoke to Alan Sears a couple of times about possibly working with Alliance Defending Freedom when I retire. Alan is the CEO, president and general counsel of ADF. We met several years ago in Colorado. He gave me the green light to continue pursuing the possibility of a job there. However, the last conversation I had with ADF about it was with a senior executive who said right now ADF doesn't want to put money into the kind of position Alan and I discussed. There were several reasons for this that all make sense. So, that door is closing.

I also check the Focus on the Family website occasionally to see what positions are available. There was one position I was half-way interested in. The website said they would begin taking applications on a particular date. I checked the website a day or two before the announcement was going to be posted, and it wasn't there anymore. So, that door is closed.

Right now, I feel very comfortable with the prospect of just waiting to see what the Lord opens up next for me. I'm never quite sure about when I should be knocking on doors and when I should be waiting. Right now, I think I wait.

It is now July 17, 2005—several months since I wrote what I did above. I received a telephone call about a month ago from Chaplain Jeff Young at the Chief of Chaplain's Office about retirement or potentially staying in the Army for another assignment. Jeff is the chaplain responsible for making assignments for chaplains who are colonels. He asked me if I would consider going to Heidelberg, Germany, to serve as one of the senior chaplains in Europe.

As a way of telling him "No," I said, "Jeff, I have an email right here from Sandy that says, 'Tell Jeff that if it isn't San Antonio, we don't want it.'" I read it to him and there was silence for about five seconds. Then he said, "I might be able to do that. We are going to assign a colonel to San Antonio fairly soon. We are not able to do so right now, but hope to be able to before too long."

After talking to Sandy and a couple of other folks familiar with San Antonio, I later talked to Jeff about it again. As of right now, if I can be assigned to San Antonio, I'll stay in the Army for another few years. If not, I'll retire. More to follow, I'm sure!

Chapter 33: Funerals Are Hard! July 2005

Samuel Manning was the son of our good friends, Bill and Petra. Bill was a fellow chaplain and colleague when we were stationed in Hawaii. Sam was born with physical problems, and, after seemingly countless procedures and surgeries, he died when he was just six and a half years old. We just returned from his funeral a few days ago.

I was on leave (military vacation time) and staying at my parents' house in Ellwood City, Pennsylvania, when Petra called me on a Saturday to tell me of Sam's death. She also asked me if I would do his funeral in Lafayette, La., the next week. Of course, I said I would.

The next day was Sunday, and Sandy and I attended mom and dad's church. I made a presentation about Alliance Defending Freedom for the adult Sunday School class, followed by preaching at the morning worship service. We then drove the 400 miles to our home at Fort Monmouth, N.J. Monday, I worked on a funeral sermon. Tuesday, we flew to Louisiana. Wednesday was Sam's funeral. Thursday, we flew home.

God's hand was evident throughout everything. We got the airline tickets free by using frequent flyer miles. The funeral was both sad and a genuine celebration—praise and worship music with guitar and bongos, balloons, and Hawaiian leis—everything Sam liked.

We had an excellent trip back to New Jersey. Due to a delay on our first flight, we were re-routed and got home almost two hours earlier than originally planned. We had perfect weather all the way. This was praiseworthy because a hurricane was working its way across the south as we traveled. A day earlier, and we would have had many delays.

Even during such tragic and sad circumstances, God provided all we needed to be with our dear friends and hopefully minister to them in their darkest hour.

Chapter 34: God Is Still In The Real Estate Business April 1, 2006

We just closed on a house in San Antonio yesterday—the house that we hope to be our retirement home and that we will live in until we die. God's hand on the whole process was quite evident.

Several months ago, I made a list of retirement concerns to pray about on a regular basis. Having a good real estate agent and buying a house was on the list. God graciously answered our prayers. A lady named Terri is our realtor; she has been understanding, very knowledgeable and extremely helpful throughout the whole process. We were referred to her through a program sponsored by my insurance company. Thank God for Terri.

We were prepared to make an offer on the house we eventually bought. The seller, however, lowered the price by $9,900 the day before we were going to make the offer. There were three offers on the place as soon as he lowered the price. Ours was the second. The people who made the first offer didn't want to close on the house for a couple of months. We were willing to close sooner and, praise God, found two mortgage companies that said they could close the house in 10 days, which would make it the end of March.

We praise God for an excellent credit rating. Because of that, the mortgage company wanted minimal documentation from us—a copy of our social security cards, a bank statement and a Leave and Earnings Statement. Had that not been the case, we would have had a very difficult time getting the required documentation because we were in Texas and all our documentation was still in New Jersey, where we lived at the time.

For the most part, we conducted the house closing via FedEx. Shortly after returning to New Jersey, I received a call letting me know that the closing documents were being emailed to me—all 89 pages. We printed them at the chapel and had no printer problems. We looked through them and went to the office of the military lawyers where an attorney was standing by to notarize them. We then made copies and immediately sent them via FedEx to my real estate agent in San Antonio. They arrived there in about 20 hours, and the house closing went off without a hitch.

Another praise has to do with my mental hang-up of signing papers or writing in front of others—don't ask me why, but I frequently get extremely nervous and am sometimes unable to write at all. This did not happen while signing all the papers to close on the house. Believe me, I know what I'm like, and this is clearly God's doing.

Chapter 35: Update On The Chapel April 2006

A quick update to what is happening at the chapel. "Feed Your Faith" is our Tuesday night program that is for all, regardless of age. We have supper together and sing a few songs before heading to our Bible studies. By God's grace, it has continued to grow. We have seven adult Bible studies, as well as both youth and children's programs. We finally reached a plateau of about 120 folks regularly attending.

God is still using the chapel to touch lives. It is something only He could do. We have used all of the available space, including the sanctuary, for classes or programs—the next place to have a Bible study would have been my office. The Deputy Chief of Chaplains, Chaplain (Brigadier General) Doug Carver was here about a month ago; he attended Tuesday evening and remarked about how evident it was that God was at work.

It is amazing how God providentially brought the right people together to lead various ministries at the chapel. I think especially of Rick and Jen Blaine, who took over the Youth of the Chapel program, and Rebekah and Shelly, who took over the Kids of the Chapel group. They are all extremely talented and dedicated to ministry. God is using them in wonderful ways.

A big concern at the chapel has been the projected turnover of the chapel staff and having the people we need to keep Feed Your Faith going. Six months ago, the picture was looking grim:

Chaplain Mike Forrester, an Army Reserve chaplain who has been on active duty, was going back to his civilian ministry in April. Rick Blaine (referred to above) will be discharged from the Army in May, and I'll be retiring—meaning we'll both be leaving at about the same time. Staff Sergeant Joseph, our non-commissioned officer in charge of the chapel, leaves in June or July. Chaplain Jack Woodford is scheduled to go to another assignment in August. Chaplain Hugh MacKenzie, another Army Reserve chaplain, returns to civilian life in August. I was told that my replacement would not arrive until mid-July, so there would be no overlap between us. All of these potential changes were very concerning.

God, however, was at work! Here is what things look like now and how things have changed: Chaplain Forrester's civilian job got cut back to 20 hours a week; he requested and received a two-year extension to stay on active duty. My replacement arrived in March and will start work in mid-April. This means there will be overlap rather than underlap; this is especially important and will help to make a smooth transition as I retire and my successor becomes the senior chaplain on post. Chaplain

Woodford is not leaving this summer. The Army has opted, for reasons unknown to me, to leave him here until next winter. Chaplain MacKenzie is also requesting, and will probably receive, a two-year extension.

I told the chapel staff at one of our meetings about six months ago that I would like them to pray about our personnel situation and that we really needed God to intervene. He did!

All of these developments were separate actions and weren't related to each other. God came through, and we now have the personnel required. Still not all that we need, but enough to keep the ministry going. I'm so thankful that God is the best personnel manager ever!

Chapter 36:
This Is What "Right" Looks Like
May 2006

I have been doing a lot of reflecting and evaluating lately. The reason is two-fold: Number one, we are leaving the Army, and number two, we are leaving Fort Monmouth. These last four years here have been, at least from my point of view, the most fruitful of my ministry. Many of the thoughts listed here were mentioned either in my retirement speech last week or at the chapel farewell. What has happened here at Fort Monmouth is truly a "God" thing.

There are two themes I've seen consistently interwoven in my life—God's providence and God's grace. This has never been more evident than while here at Fort Monmouth. I think the turning point of our four years here was the "40 Days of Purpose" campaign we conducted in the fall of 2003. In hindsight, we can clearly see God's hand in it all.

Jolanthe Bassett, one of our parishioners, first brought the idea to me. We thought about it, prayed about it and decided we would do it. Shirley Simmons, another parishioner, soon agreed to be our campaign director.

I couldn't have asked for a better director. God then provided a leadership team in the form of Debbe Smith, Mike Pettitt, Lori Sorrels, Charlie Spears and Joel Day. Many others came on board on various teams; I have never seen the Body of Christ function more like it is designed to function than here at Fort Monmouth.

Another aspect of God putting people into place was Peter Oglesby. My full-time secretary, Debbie Menninger, was pregnant. Like many offices, Debbie was the one who really knew what was going on and, in many ways, was the glue that held things together. Due to physical concerns, Debbie had to quit work until she had her baby. With the "40 Days" campaign on the horizon, her absence left a huge hole in our office, and God then provided Peter Oglesby for us.

Peter attended the Catholic mass and our Tuesday night program. His training was in television production. He not only did a particularly good job of taking over for Debbie in our office, but he was invaluable in providing audiovisual support and ideas for the campaign. After "40 Days of Purpose" ended, his contribution culminated in an excellent 16-minute video that highlighted the various aspects of the campaign.

God richly blessed the campaign with several new Christians, folks who wanted to be baptized, and a host of others getting off the sidelines and into the game—becoming active in chapel life like they never had before. Many were discovering God's purpose for their lives for the first time.

An example of what God had done could be seen in our "Feed Your Faith" program on Tuesday evenings. Prior to the campaign, we had one Tuesday night Bible study with about 15 people attending. We are now averaging 120 who are spread out among seven adult Bible studies, a dynamic Kids of the Chapel program and an equally dynamic Protestant Youth of the Chapel.

God energized and brought His people together in a "God-like" fashion. We used to wonder where we would get teachers. We now have teachers ready and waiting for the chance to teach. We used to have to scrounge around for volunteers or teenagers to take care of the kids' programs. First, God provided Rebekah Miklos, who did a wonderful job. Then, he provided Shelly Phillips, who raised the bar even higher. We went from a poor Protestant Youth of the Chapel program to an excellent one with a strong spiritual focus thanks to God providing Rick and Jen Blaine.

So much of what happened at Fort Monmouth can be capsulated in a conversation I had a couple of months ago with Chaplain (Brigadier General) Doug Carver, Deputy Chief of Chaplains. At the time, Doug was the second highest rank a chaplain could achieve; he would eventually go on to get promoted to major general and become the Chief of Chaplains, the Army's senior chaplain. Attending the Chaplain Advance Course together in 1987, I'd known Chaplain Carver for almost 20 years. I had invited him to come and speak at our Fort Monmouth National Prayer Breakfast. He flew in from Washington, D.C., on a Tuesday afternoon, attended "Feed Your Faith" on Tuesday evening and spoke at the prayer breakfast Wednesday morning. I then gave him a formal military briefing about Fort Monmouth. He made three comments that are worth documenting here:

1). We were eating dinner at "Feed Your Faith" when he asked me who various people were. He said that in his entire career as a military chaplain, he'd never seen a chapel program like this, with so many people excited about what God was doing and wanting be part of it.

2). Later, we walked down the hall and saw the various classes. As we visited a couple of them, I pointed out different folks and explained to him that some were from the Protestant congregation, some were from the Catholic congregation and others came from the Baptist church in Red Bank, the Methodist church in Ocean Grove or another local civilian church. Among other things, he was impressed by the fact that folks from civilian churches were attending an activity at a military chapel because of the spiritual nurturing they were receiving. As we were walking down the hall, he stopped, looked at me and said, "Brother, God is at work here."

3). He was speaking to the chapel staff after the briefing I gave the next day when he said, "This is what 'right' looks like." I took his words to heart, thinking that God was at work and that when God does something, He does it right.

What a blessing it was to be at Fort Monmouth during this time and to witness what God was doing.

Hallelujah!

Chapter 37: An Ice Storm In Texas? January 16, 2007

We have been procrastinating about buying cell phones—but the last couple of days I wish we hadn't put off doing so. I spent last night in Austin after attending a briefing sponsored by the Texas Restoration Project. We had some bad weather the day before yesterday when I drove to Austin, and it got much worse while I was there. The weatherman on the news said it was the worst ice storm on record in San Antonio. The city was basically shut down, with many roads closed.

I got ready to leave Austin to return to San Antonio today and wasn't sure the best time to leave. I was done at the conference by 9 a.m., but could stay in my room until 1 p.m. The weather was already bad, and I didn't know whether to leave immediately or wait until it hopefully warmed up a little.

Sandy wanted me to find another motel, but I wanted to get back to San Antonio. My concern was threefold. For starters, Texans aren't used to this weather, and many don't know how to drive in it. Secondly, some roads were backed-up due to accidents, including I-35—which was the interstate I would need to take home. Finally, I-35 through Austin had many elevated roads, bridges and overpasses where the ice would form more quickly than on other streets.

As I loaded my car, I began talking to a hotel employee who was putting salt on the sidewalk. He asked what route I was taking and suggested I take a different route than I had planned to use to get back to I-35. The route he suggested avoided elevated roads, bridges and overpasses. It also put me on I-35 much further south, which was the direction I would be heading. Following his advice, I was able to avoid the most dangerous parts of the various roads, and I had no problems getting home. Praise God!

As I was leaving the hotel, I noticed a man scraping the ice off his car with a credit card. What Yankee hasn't done that? I offered him my ice scraper; this delayed me by about 10 minutes. It turned out that if I had left immediately, I would have been stuck in a traffic jam as I headed south on I-35. Not offering him my ice scraper would have put me in the traffic jam.

The trip from Austin to home took about five hours, more than twice as long as it would normally have taken. By God's grace, I made it home safely. Sandy and I were both very thankful for God's provision and guidance along the way. We only had one car at that time, and I obviously had it. Following this experience—we now have two cars and two cell phones.

Hallelujah!

Chapter 38: Hawaiian Island Ministry Conference April 5, 2008

Sandy and I just left the Hawaiian Island Ministry (HIM) conference and came back to the Hale Koa a few minutes ago. I thought I'd take a few minutes to write down some thoughts about it. HIM is an annual, three-day, two-night, non-denominational conference.

For starters, the entire conference was great! I sensed the Lord's presence throughout. For some reason, I was very emotional and had tears in my eyes at almost every service. I feel like the Lord really enforced some things in my heart through the speakers.

One young man spoke about ministering to the homeless, the poor and the needy. His message was particularly challenging as I'm trying to develop a more biblical worldview in my own life. Paul Shepherd spoke three times and all three messages ministered to me. The first message was about Hannah from chapter one of I Samuel. He talked about Hannah's emptiness of soul being something that God put there; the emptiness caused her to seek the Lord. He also talked about how Hannah's husband, Elkanah, "didn't get it." In other words, he didn't understand her emptiness.

I especially identified with the first point—the aspect of emptiness. I've said for quite a while that I'm still trying to find my purpose in life since retiring from the Army. I'm not sure Sandy realizes the sense of emptiness inside me. I don't know if she can understand since her day-to-day life hasn't changed as much as mine has since we retired.

Paul Shepherd also spoke about destiny and diligence. In other words, God's sovereignty and human responsibility. He took his teaching from the book of Ruth. I can also identify with this. I came away from his teaching convinced I need to continue studying various passages of scripture dealing with impacting our culture. I think right now studying is my responsibility—how I then use what I learned is God's.

This was confirmed in Tony Evan's message this afternoon on David and Goliath. He said that David's responsibility was to pick up the five stones and go and meet Goliath. God was ready to bring Goliath down; He just needed David to do his part. I think my part right now is to continue studying and trust God to show me the avenue for doing something with what I've learned.

Paul Shepherd's teaching this morning was about times and seasons in our lives. He said there are primarily four seasons: preparation, sowing, waiting and reaping. From his explanation, I would say that right now I'm in the waiting season. He said this can be characterized sometimes by confusion and questions; that's me right now. I just trust that the season of reaping will come along soon.

A man named Ken Medema was a great inspiration. A blind man, he composes songs—including the notes he plays on the piano on the spot right after each presentation. The songs he composes are a recap of the message. Absolutely outstanding!

The HIM conference has given me a newness and freshness and has invigorated me to keep on keeping on. I feel cleansed! Praise God!

Chapter 39: The God Of Technology May 3, 2008

I got a new Dell laptop in January and have been having problems with it lately. I've called the folks at Dell customer support several times; after each call, the computer will be OK for a few days but then another problem would develop. I just got back from Chaplain Interaction 2008, and the only way I could even get it to turn on was by pressing the power button and then immediately pressing the F8 button several times to get it on. It would then work OK—not great, but OK.

I am really hoping to use the laptop for ministry—being able to take it with me to various places and do things on it. Yesterday morning, during my prayer time, I prayed for the laptop. I then downloaded and installed the Vista Service Pack One, which apparently was just made available. Part of that installation process is reconfiguring the settings. Praise God, as of right now, the laptop is working perfectly.

Chapter 40: Ministry To Internationals May 4, 2008

Sandy and I just returned from Chaplain Interaction 2008 a few days ago. It was conducted at Fort Bliss, an Army base in El Paso, Texas. Chaplain Interaction is sponsored by the Association for Christian Conferences, Teaching and Service (ACCTS). Last year was the first year, and the plan is for it to become an annual event.

ACCTS brings military Christians from around the globe to the States for two weeks of training on how to minister in the military setting. It was a wonderful, God-blessed experience. We had delegates from seven different foreign countries—Madagascar, Bangladesh, Moldova, Papua New Guinea, Guatemala, Zambia and Namibia. Five of the men brought their wives. Here are just a few of the ways God was with us and blessed us during this experience:

I became aware, possibly as never before, of how great and glorious God's Church is. We were with wonderful believers who were encouraging in many ways. His Church truly is greater than any denomination, color, creed, gender or any other possible barrier or difference.

We spent about two hours one evening sharing stories and testimonies. How encouraging that was—to see what God was doing in the lives of His people around the world. It was also exceptionally uplifting to see the commitment of these good folks to Him. Some are living and working for Him in very difficult situations. I think of one couple from Moldova; the testimonies they shared of God at work were tremendous. There is also Juan from Guatemala, a chaplain laboring in a difficult situation. Guatemala has a new chaplaincy, and it is still going through some growing pains. Despite the difficulties, Juan ministers with a smile on his face and a commitment to the soldiers.

We went to Cloudcroft, N.M., for a couple days for a marriage retreat. God helped us get past border patrol agents in New Mexico; I didn't expect to see them there because we had traveled quite a distance from the Mexican border. The agent gave us a lecture because some of the delegates didn't have their passports or visas with them, but he did let us through. God also protected us from what could have been a bad accident. Our driver of a 15-passenger van, a chaplain assistant stationed at Fort Bliss, pulled out in front of at least three vehicles on a highway. They swerved around us, gave us dirty looks, but did not hit us. Praise God!

I also got what we think was food poisoning one night; I had diarrhea and was throwing up. I didn't sleep well at all that night and was responsible for four classes the next day. While my stomach felt somewhat better, I was very tired and totally washed out—probably dehydrated too. Praise God, however, that I was able to get through the day. After classes, I went back to our room, slept for an hour and woke up feeling fine. The next day I was back to feeling 100 percent.

God also gave us an absolutely blessed time for our closing ceremony. We started off singing praise choruses, which were followed by testimonies from the delegates. I then gave a devotional. We ended with a communion service and the giving of attendance certificates. God visited us during communion. Some were taking communion in the pews while others came to the altar. One gal at the altar spontaneously began singing "Just As I Am" a capella, and others joined in. Then we sang "Let Us Break Bread Together" followed by "Amazing Grace." God truly blessed us with a sense of His presence—not in an overly joyful, hand-clapping way—we just knew He was there! It was fantastic, and I will remember it for a long time.

Chaplain Interaction is a wonderful ministry to some wonderful people. May God be glorified! We were blessed to be part of it for more than 10 years.

Sandy and me with representatives from Namibia, Papua New Guinea, Moldova, Zambia, Madagascar, Bangladesh and Guatemala.

Chapter 41: Radiator Light And A Long Trip August 3, 2008

I am writing right now from Kelly and Sarah's house in Jacksonville, Texas. We are on our way back to San Antonio after a trip of five and a half weeks and more than 5,000 miles. As usual, our van is loaded down with all kinds of stuff. We also have Bailey, our cocker spaniel, with us.

Leaving Ellwood City, Pennsylvania, to begin our journey back to Texas, we had only gone about five miles when my radiator light came on signifying the van was overheating. I immediately turned the van off for a few minutes and went back to a mechanic I trusted in Ellwood City; this is the same mechanic my dad uses. He looked at the van and told me I had a small leak somewhere that probably just leaked when the van was turned off after running. We filled the radiator up again, and we were on our way.

I've had to add fluid to the radiator every morning. Doing this got us all the way to Jacksonville, Texas, without a problem. The leak has gotten a little worse since getting here, and we're going to take the van to the mechanic tomorrow before going back home to San Antonio.

We are extremely thankful the radiator light went on while we were still close enough to Ellwood City to get a diagnosis rather than the light coming on once we were miles away or even on a freeway. Thank You, Lord!

Chapter 42: Cradled In God's Arms July 2009

I've gotten more claustrophobic as I've gotten older. So much so, that I sometimes almost talk myself into it, especially if I know I have an elevator ride in my near future or another circumstance that could cause claustrophobia. This has bothered me to the extent that I asked the VA (Veterans Affairs) doctor for something for claustrophobia. He gave me some Xanax.

I was flying to Pittsburgh a couple of weeks ago and had thought about it beforehand so much that I fully expected to get claustrophobic during my flight. I got on the plane, put my backpack in the overhead and sat in my seat. I immediately began feeling like the claustrophobia was coming on. I got up, opened the Xanax bottle and took one out. I put it in my pocket and sat down without taking it. I also took a few deep breaths and prayed. I calmed down some but still wasn't sure I wouldn't take the pill.

The plane began to taxi down the runway for takeoff when I laid my head back and began praying again. Almost immediately, I began to feel drowsy and drifted off to sleep a little. When I woke up, there was absolutely no sense of claustrophobia. I enjoyed that flight to Atlanta, and after changing planes there, enjoyed the next one to Pittsburgh—without even a hint of claustrophobia. I flew home two weeks later with no sense of claustrophobia at all. There is no way to explain what happened to me. It was like God just cradled me in His arms, took away any fear or claustrophobia at all and bathed me in His presence.

I never did take the pill.

Chapter 43: Dead Batteries And Vans That Won't Run July 2009

We just got back a few days ago from a family cruise to Progresso and Cozumel. The cruise left out of the port in Galveston, Texas. God had his hand in getting us there. The original plan was for us to drive our van from San Antonio to our motel in Texas City; we would meet Kelly and Sarah there. Then Kelly and I planned to take the van back to the Houston airport where we would pick up Casey and his family.

The van's battery went dead about five days before we were supposed to leave; this was a 60-month battery that we only had for 27 months. I got a new battery and wanted to drive the van as much as possible to make sure that if it had any problems, we would know it before we left—I didn't want to have problems on the highway going to Galveston. I am glad I did, because the van then began having a very different kind of problem the day after getting the new battery; it was idling badly and the engine didn't run smoothly at all.

I immediately took it to the garage. They looked at it, spent some time trying to determine the problem and told me what they needed to do to fix it. I explained we were on a timeline to get it back and why I needed it. The owner of the garage said he would do all he could to get it fixed and back it to me.

He called me back the day before we were to leave to tell me that the problem was worse than they thought. The van needed a new main computer, and it would take him four or five days to get one in. Also, of course, it would be much more expensive.

All of that is a God thing. Thank God the battery went dead when it did—that is what caused me to drive the van more frequently than I normally would, which is when I caught the poor idling and the van not running smoothly. With the van unable to make the trip, we instead took our car and did not have to worry about the van surviving the trip.

We met Kelly and Sarah at the Houston airport rather than in Texas City. With Casey and family in our car, we all then drove to the motel there. Our original plan of going to Texas City first and then going to the airport would have been a mess. We didn't realize how far Texas City was from the Houston airport, and we were driving during rush-hour traffic. So, praise God for dead batteries and vans that won't run.

Sandy and me with (l. to r.) Casey, Darcie,
Braden, Ashton, Sarah and Kelly
on our cruise.

Chapter 44: IAEC Trip To Bulgaria (Part 1) October 2009

I've been back from Bulgaria for about 36 hours and am starting some much-needed time of reflection. The trip was a whirlwind, so now I need to sit down and reflect on it and the things I'm aware of that God has done. Not only do I think He worked through our team (Bulgarian and U.S.), but I can't remember a time in my life when He has worked in *me* to the extent that He has recently—teaching me and revealing Himself to me. Those are the things I hope I don't miss.

This was my first trip overseas with the International Association of Evangelical Chaplains (IAEC). IAEC's mission is to "encourage, equip, and empower evangelicals worldwide who are involved in military ministry." In Bulgaria, this means we conducted five full days of training with five or six men involved in military ministry. All members of IAEC's Board of Directors, as well as the trainers, are retired military. Our American team for Bulgaria was me, Bernie Windmiller (a retired Army chaplain) and Clay Buckingham (a retired armor officer).

Ironically, our U.S. team had the feeling this was going to be a good trip because of what we considered to be the spiritual warfare taking place before the trip. I am not one of those people who sees a demon behind every problem, but it seemed that Satan was doing whatever he could to stop the trip from taking place—or at least to impact it in a negative way. This took a couple of different forms for me. One was a urinary tract infection (UTI) that sent me to an urgent care clinic. My last UTI, several years ago, resulted in missing almost three months of work and resulted in surgery before I could return to work. So, the UTI had us concerned.

The next thing was a call from my mom and dad's doctor saying they needed to be in an assisted-living facility immediately. That meant shifting mental gears, making a week-long unplanned trip to Pennsylvania and entering the new world of assisted living—something I knew nothing about. It has been stressful and has required a big learning curve for me; there were decisions to make, logistical concerns to consider, emotional issues of putting mom and dad in the facility to deal with and other family issues to decide, as well as questions about what to do with their house, their stuff, etc.

I remember calling Bernie Windmiller one Saturday afternoon and telling him everything that was going on. At this point, we had not yet received the training schedule, so I asked him if I could teach classes I had already prepared since, with the unplanned trip to Pennsylvania, I wouldn't have time to prepare new ones. He graciously agreed.

I went to Pennsylvania to work on the assisted-living issue and, while there, made another trip to the urgent care clinic—this time with bronchitis. Praise God, however, my sister and I did find mom and dad an assisted-living facility we thought would be good. I fly back to Pennsylvania next week to move them in.

These things I've mentioned don't even include the problems with our minivan (six weeks in the shop at a cost of $3,000), plumbing problems that cost another $700 or having to buy a new lawnmower and a new washer. On top of all of this, my mom spent some time in the hospital, and I began taking on new responsibilities at our church. This teaches me that God does indeed have a sense of humor—all of this took place while I was studying the Book of Job, which I still am.

Just prior to the trip to Pennsylvania was a two-day trip to the Army Chaplain School at Fort Jackson, S.C. I had four days at home between South Carolina and Pennsylvania and four days at home between Pennsylvania and Bulgaria. This was a stressful time since I was always packing or unpacking and thinking about where I'd been or where I was going. I also still had my responsibilities at home, including trying to be a good husband, which I'm not sure I did a very good job of.

I left for Bulgaria on a Sunday morning. I felt from the very beginning that it would be a good trip. I was able to get my seat changed to an aisle seat on an exit row from San Antonio to Chicago. With the change of seats, "it just so happened" that I was seated beside a lady who was a

Christian. We began talking about where I was going and what I was going to do. As we landed in Chicago, she took my hands in hers and prayed for me. She said she was going home and would look up Yambol on the Internet to see where it was and that she would pray for us throughout the week.

I called Sandy from the Chicago airport, where I was supposed to link up with Bernie. She told me she had received a call from Bernie's wife, and that he had been taken to the emergency room the night before and probably wouldn't make the trip. I called Bernie at the hospital and had prayer with him over the phone. Realizing he wouldn't be joining us, my first thought was that—while this was unexpected from my point of view, this turn of events didn't surprise Go—and that it would be exciting to see how He worked things out and what He did. I wasn't disappointed.

While walking down the jetway and onto my plane in Chicago, I remember thinking that I was now walking by faith and not by sight. Because Bernie had made all the arrangements, I wasn't sure who was going to meet my airplane in Sofia, Bulgaria. I had never met, spoken with, or emailed Mladen or Svetlana. Mladen was our point of contact and host, the person Bernie had coordinated everything with. This included the training. Svetlana was our primary translator.

I knew I would be landing in Sofia, and it was about 200 miles from Yambol, where we were to conduct the training. I prayed someone would be at the airport to meet me when I landed. Praise God that Mladen was standing there holding a sign with my name on it. We linked up and took off for the 200-mile drive to Yambol.

I don't remember exactly what event triggered the thought, but I just began thinking about how big God really is and how my vision and understanding of Him needs to be enlarged. That thought stayed with me for the next few days—just how big God really is.

We arrived at my hotel, and I immediately had a meeting with Clay and Clara Buckingham, who had taken the train from Romania where they had been visiting mutual friends. Clay and I would be co-teachers for the week; we had to decide who would teach Bernie's classes, since he couldn't make the trip. With that completed, I finally got to bed after traveling for close to 30 hours. I was scheduled to teach the first class at 8:00 a.m. the next morning.

The first couple of days were difficult for me, primarily due to jet lag, I think. My body ached, I was very tired and my intestinal tract wasn't keeping up with the time change. Praise God I never got sick, but I didn't feel like eating for a few days, so I ate very little. I kept thinking "I can't do this." I was just too tired and felt cruddy all over.

My sleeping was really messed up, but the Holy Spirit brought Scripture to my mind as I laid awake wishing I could go back to sleep. The passage was II Corinthians 12:9: "My grace is sufficient for you. My power is made perfect in your weakness." I am so thankful for the Holy Spirit reminding me of that verse. It helped me realize in a way I had not realized before that this was God's work. It was His power, as shown through my weakness, that would accomplish His purposes for the training. I also realized His grace was sufficient for me for whatever I was called upon to do.

God was definitely working in me. I still wanted to feel better, get over the jet lag and have my appetite return, but my feelings and what I wanted weren't as important anymore. God had given me the desire for His power to be made perfect in me. If that meant I was tired and didn't feel well, that's OK—His grace is sufficient.

God blessed the week of training. We all learned from each other and were strengthened and blessed as we experienced Christian love and unity that transcends culture and language. I spoke at the church's Wednesday evening service. The response from the people who attended was very good. Praise God for the power of His Word and for Svetlana, an excellent translator. We then finished the rest of the training on Saturday, and I preached the Sunday morning service.

Sunday evening, the night before driving to Sofia to speak at a military academy, I spent another night of lying in bed for a couple of hours in the middle of the night without sleep. The chorus that kept going through my mind has the words "Emmanuel—God with us." I realized God was reminding me that He would be with us throughout the events of the next day.

Chapter 45: IAEC Trip To Bulgaria (Part 2) October 2009

As seen in the previous chapter, God's hand was evident both before our training in Bulgaria and during the training. But He wasn't done blessing us or making himself known though. I still had several days in Bulgaria with more ministry opportunities.

Monday morning, we drove to Sofia and went to the military academy. At first, we didn't know if I would be allowed to speak since the initial request was for Bernie and the academy requires 20 days' notice for any changes to be made; we were about five days away when we requested the substitution. Mladen, who had served in the Bulgarian military, used the word "miracle" to describe what happened when the approval came through. I knew this was a big deal because of how excited and happy he was when he got the word I could speak.

For my briefing, I answered the question, "what in the world is a chaplain?" To answer it, I simply talked about what chaplains do, and it was received very well. The deputy commander talked to the students before the briefing about how their military needed a chaplain ministry. Having received a more accurate view of the chaplaincy, he was even more adamant about this after the briefing. He invited me back to speak at the academy the next time I am in Bulgaria. Mladen said that maybe the reason they approved me to speak was because they know they need a chaplaincy and are hungry for more information about it.

Mladen, Svetlana and I went out to eat after the briefing and were considering how to get the law changed in Bulgaria so there could be religious freedom on military bases and chaplains could be authorized. At the present time, the only ministry allowed is performed by orthodox priests. As the three of us discussed this, Mladen received a call telling him that we had been added to the calendar of the chairman of one of the four leading political parties in Bulgaria. The purpose of the meeting would be to talk about chaplaincy. Talk about a "God thing!"

I didn't realize it at the time, but I see now that Satan did not want us to minister in Sofia. Mladen's son, Presley, was not only sick with a cough and a fever but burned both of his hands badly on a stove in the house the day before we were to go to Sofia. Because of this, Mladen couldn't spend much time with us Sunday and it was "iffy" whether he would make the trip to Sofia on Monday. If he didn't, Svetlana and I would have to make the trip alone and fulfill the commitments with all my luggage by taking buses, trains and taxis. Praise God that Mladen did make the trip with their van and that Presley is continuing to improve.

I am not positive how this time with the chairman came about. Svetlana's cousin is a politician in Yambol, and we are guessing he set it up. I don't know how he was aware of what we were doing, but I do know that Mladen and Svetlana were quite excited—as this appointment was unexpected.

I experienced one more night with difficulty sleeping, and God came through again with another chorus—this time through the words of the chorus, "In Christ Alone." The words that kept going through my mind were "From life's first cry to final breath, Jesus commands my destiny." I began thinking about this and was amazed by the Providence of God in what was happening. The next day I shared with Mladen and Svetlana how I believe God had, from eternity past, for some reason known only to Him, chosen the three of us and, in His Sovereign plan, brought us together on this particular day to speak to the chairman. Together, we began looking at God's Hand in some of the things that were occurring.

Our training ended Saturday. "It just so happened" that I hadn't made reservations to fly home until Wednesday. The time with the chairman was Tuesday afternoon at 4:00 p.m. I flew out Wednesday morning at 6:00 a.m.

"It just so happened" that Bernie didn't come and that he couldn't have met with the chairman if he had come because of when his flight was scheduled to leave Bulgaria.

"It just so happened" that someone apparently called Svetlana's cousin to see if he could get us an appointment with the chairman of the political party.

"It just so happened" that we got the last-minute approval to speak at the academy.

We were amazed and humbled to think that for some reason God brought us all together and had chosen us to speak to someone in a position of authority. As humbling as that thought was, we also talked about the fact that we could speak respectfully, but boldly, about the need for religious freedom and chaplaincy for the military. The Lord also gave me the opportunity to do the same thing during a 30-minute radio interview.

We met with the chairman and one of his staff the next afternoon. The chairman explained that he is supportive of the military chaplaincy, but things take time and all new proposals to parliament had to be made by next Monday, six days away. We spoke to him for a few minutes and provided him with a broader and more accurate view of the chaplaincy, which he said he appreciated. I learned that many folks look at the chaplain as only doing religious services and are unaware of the broad practical aspects of the chaplaincy. The chairman gave us a point of contact for the future, we took a picture and left.

About 45 minutes later, we got a call from the chairman's office asking us for more information about the chaplaincy. He said he needed it in the next few days because they wanted to offer a proposal to parliament next Monday. I am sure this is a slow process, but I believe God has been involved in this and is beginning to break down the walls of resistance so there might be religious freedom in the Bulgarian military. We praise God for this unexpected divine appointment with the chairman.

I am convinced God is doing a work in Bulgaria and that He will bring religious freedom to the military. I think of William Wilberforce and his years of unrelenting hard work to abolish slavery in England. By God's grace, He will bring about religious freedom for the military of Bulgaria and will establish a chaplaincy including evangelical chaplains.

I have never had an experience like I did in Bulgaria. Despite the obstacles (dealing with jet lag, not feeling like eating, etc.), I have never felt so completely in the center of God's will as I did during this trip. I feel like I was confronted with the reality of God. I realize that is as basic as you can get, but I don't know how else to say it. God is . . . and He is who He says He is! I continue to be astonished at God's grace and at His sovereign plan.

Clay and Clara Buckingham and I, along with the rest of our class, in Yambol, Bulgaria.

With Svetlana, our lead translator.

Chapter 46: Mom's Death June 2009–June 2010

Mom and dad had been going downhill for a while when my sister, Kyle, and I decided we needed to get some help for them. We began asking around, and a friend who is a nurse in Ellwood City mentioned the Beaver County Office for Aging (BCOA). I contacted them. The paperwork I needed to complete for BCOA was frustrating, time-consuming and tedious. It included many hours of going through seemingly countless files trying to find information regarding insurance policies, mutual funds, taxes, savings and social security payments, and compiling all of mom and dad's expenses.

It was an incredible task after mom and dad had gathered paperwork for 60 years and seemingly thrown little of it away. Not to mention that the paperwork had been kept in various and unusual places throughout the house, including in the kitchen, bedroom and even the basement. Added to all of this was the fact that I live in Texas and had to make frequent trips to Pennsylvania to deal with this. All of that said, finding all of the documentation I just mentioned paid big dividends later in ways we did not anticipate.

We were able to get through the paperwork process for BCOA and received approval for mom and dad to have some housekeeping done, get some help with medicines and receive other assistance. After doing all of that, however, my folks declined the help because they didn't want to spend the money. I couldn't talk them into it.

I got a call from Dr. Swamy, mom and dad's family doctor, sometime in September 2009 saying my folks needed to be in assisted living. This is the call I'd been waiting for, and I praise God for it. This is because in my mom and dad's eyes, it was their doctor who was then the "bad guy" rather than Kyle or me. Had they looked at either of us that way, it would have made things more difficult moving forward.

So, another trip to Pennsylvania was needed for me to find a place for them to go. After looking around and visiting several facilities, we decided on Katera's Kove and moved mom and dad in on Nov. 1, 2009. It was about a 10-minute drive from my sister Kyle's house, so she and other friends could visit regularly and take them places.

Praise God for all of the work I'd previously done organizing their paperwork, because it came in extremely helpful when applying for Aid & Attendance with the Veteran's Administration (VA), as well as filing out the application for them to go to Katera's Kove. Aid & Attendance is a

VA benefit for wartime veterans. Once approved, the veteran gets monthly financial assistance to help with long-term care. Thankfully, dad was approved for this. As of today (July 1, 2010), although the VA still owes us some retroactive pay, dad is receiving a monthly check that made it possible for them to be at Katera's Kove.

Mom and dad also put their house in my and Kyle's names two years ago. Praise God that this had been done when it was. While that had its challenges, trying to put it in our names now would be even more difficult.

I am currently traveling a lot with a parachurch ministry named the International Association of Evangelical Chaplains; this means Sandy and I have to plan out our schedule months ahead. The fact that I was here with her six days before mom died was providential. I was scheduled to speak at a small camp in Fairmont, West Virginia, the week of July 4-9. As I had during the last couple of years, we decided to visit family in Pennsylvania prior to going to Fairmont. Since we were doing that, Sandy and her sister, Judi, pulled together a surprise party for their mom and dad's 60th anniversary while we are here.

I got a call from mom's doctor, Dr. Swamy, the day after we started driving from Texas to Pennsylvania. He told me that mom was being placed on hospice. I told him that when I thought of hospice, I thought of someone who maybe had only three to six months to live. He said, "if even that long."

We pulled into Pennsylvania on Sunday, June 20. We went straight to Katera's Kove where "it just so happened" that Kyle was beginning a meeting with the nurse from hospice. She told us she thought mom had about a week left. Because of the providential planning of the trip, I was able to be with mom the last six days of her life, and we were able to be part of the anniversary party for Sandy's mom and dad.

My last conversation with mom was a beautiful gift from God. I was in the room with her by myself. She had her eyes closed most of the time but did open them occasionally. I asked her if she wanted to say the Lord's Prayer with me. When I was done saying it, she faintly—but audibly and understandably—kept repeating "Glory . . . glory . . . glory . . . glory." After she stopped, I gave her a kiss on the forehead and told her I loved her. I then put my cheek next to her mouth and asked her if she could give me a kiss. She did. That was our last real communication.

The fact that I'd done all the paperwork preparation last summer is really paying off now. Without having previously completed it, I'd be struggling now to find all the information I need regarding points of contact for life insurance, investments, the VA, etc. Praise God again that all that work had already been done.

I just returned from Romania and Bulgaria a month ago. I'm scheduled to return to Bulgaria in September. I was concerned about whether I'd be able to make that trip when I heard mom was put on hospice, since we didn't know how long she would live. I had a meeting with a couple of friends when we drove through Memphis, Tenn., on our way to Pennsylvania. We had prayer together at the end of the meeting with both of them praying for God's perfect timing in her death and to help me to make good decisions regarding going to Bulgaria or trying to get someone to go in my place. God answered this prayer for us, and her death won't hinder my participation.

My prayer for mom had changed over the last month or so. I was now praying the words of Psalm 139:16, "all the days ordained for me were written in your book before one of them came to be." I began praying for God's perfect timing in mom's death and that He would help us adjust to it.

I was listening to a Travis Cottrell CD while driving to Katera's Kove the morning of June 26. It was a beautiful morning. The song "In Christ Alone" came on. The words "from life's first cry to final breath, Jesus commands my destiny" again spoke to me and brought tears to my eyes as I worshipped. I began feeling as though God was telling me that this would be the day mom died. It was—and it was a beautiful day for mom to go to heaven.

Sometime during the day before she died, I took a few minutes to go into mom's room by myself and to talk to her. Although I'm unsure of what she could hear and/or comprehend, I told her that I loved her, and that it was OK if she wanted to go to be with Jesus and her mother, father, brothers and sister. I then had prayer with her; she died about 9:30 p.m. that night.

As I look back over the events of the last year, God's hand is written all over everything: the paperwork; the selection of Katera's Kove; the timing of our trip to Pennsylvania; the planning of the anniversary party; the timing of the hospice meeting—and many other things I can't remember or don't recognize right now.

Another, but especially important, aspect of mom's death is the financial aspect of it. The fact that she died before my dad is significant. To pay for Katera's Kove required her Social Security, his Social Security, his pension, his Aid & Attendance from the VA, plus about $1,000 a month from their savings. When dad retired years earlier, they had two options for receiving his pension. Option No. 1 was a larger pension, but mom wouldn't get any further checks when he died. Option No. 2 was a smaller pension, but mom would continue to get some money when he died.

They had chosen Option No. 1. This meant that if dad had died first, mom would have received no money except Social Security and a reduced Aid & Attendance. Had he died first, I don't know how we could have afforded for her to stay at Katera's Kove. I'm not sure what would have happened to mom or how we would have cared for her. With her dying first, my dad should be able to stay there the rest of his life without any financial problems. We definitely see God's hand in mom dying first.

Chapter 47: Make This Beeping Stop! July 11, 2010

We were on the first day of our trip from Pennsylvania back to Texas following mom's death when I stopped at a rest area in Kentucky so we could take a quick break and change drivers. Sandy and Bailey (our dog) stayed in the car while I went to the restroom. Sandy locked the car when I got out. When I came back to the car, I stuck my hand through the window, which was down, to unlock the car door. The car alarm (the horn continually beeping) activated. It continued to beep while we tried to figure out how to get it to stop.

We tried the panic buttons on our keys, we turned the car on and off, we locked and unlocked it on the inside of the door—nothing would stop it from beeping. We were both getting frustrated and concerned that we wouldn't be able to get it to stop. Sandy gave me the owner's manual and I was beginning to look through it when a lady pulled up beside us; she worked for Mazda and knew about this stuff. I gave her the keys, she put them in the driver's side door and turned them. The beeping stopped!

I don't remember exactly when, but at some point during the confusion, Sandy said something about God. I am convinced the Mazda lady showing up and parking beside us was God's provision and how He took care of us when we didn't have a clue. What are the chances that on a busy freeway a lady who knows something about car security systems "just so happens" to get off the freeway when we're having trouble and "just so happens" to park right beside us?

Thank you, Lord!

Chapter 48: Fifty-Four Years Of Stuff April 2011

There aren't very many things in life that I "hate the thought of," but cleaning out mom and dad's house was one of them. They lived in the house for 54 years, and, while I'm sure they had gotten rid of many things over the years, there was still tons of stuff that something needed to be done with.

I set aside 10 days in April to clean it all out; my goal at the end of those 10 days was to have the house completely empty. Kyle, my sister, had a dumpster delivered and I coordinated a pick-up with the Salvation Army in Pittsburgh in preparation for moving all of their stuff out. I also hoped to make some headway toward putting a new sidewalk in the backyard and even replacing the bathroom floor. How naïve I was!

I really had no idea what I was in for. Walking around the house and looking into closets, cubbyholes, under the steps, etc.—I couldn't believe it. I had been told the attic was already cleaned out; it wasn't. I felt as overwhelmed as I have ever been. The first night I literally sat down on the basement floor and cried.

I had called Jim Houk, a good friend of dad's, the week before I went to Pennsylvania to get some points of contact for the concrete and the bathroom floor. Jim had owned and rented out about 10 houses locally and knew all the places that did the things I needed to have done. He called me the day after I got to Pennsylvania and gave me a couple of names. He also said he'd stop by the house sometime when I was there.

He did so the next day and then spent the better part of the next six or seven days helping me empty the house. He was interested in a lot of the things to take to a local auction, so we loaded what he wanted into his pick-up truck and a trailer he had. The things he didn't want, we threw into a dumpster. By the end of the week, we had filled three dumpsters. Jim even helped me clean out the attic. When the Salvation Army came, the only thing left was a couch and a chair.

Cleaning out the house **absolutely could not have happened** if God hadn't sent Jim to help me. His help was totally unexpected. God knew my need and met it in a wonderful way!

Chapter 49: The Big Do-Over August 2011

I wrote in April of this year, just a few months ago, how God provided Jim Houk to help me clean out the house. That was major, but not all that needed to be done. The next thing to do was to fix up the house so it could be rented and eventually sold.

God provided my cousin Brenda for this. She is not only very good at looking at a place and understanding what needs to be done and knowing what would look good, but she is also talented and experienced when it comes to actually doing a lot of the work herself.

Brenda and I looked at the house when I was in Pennsylvania in June to see what needed to be repaired or replaced. A partial list includes: pulling up all the carpeting; re-installing the hardwood floors; painting the walls and ceilings; installing new registers, a new bathtub and a couple of new fixtures; moving the washer and dryer to the basement; and putting in new floors in the kitchen, dining room and bathroom. To be honest, there's even more than that.

I hired Brenda to either do all of this work herself or to act as a sub-contractor and find someone she trusted to do it. As of today, it has cost about $10,000 but I'm told the house is beautiful. Brenda also had a friend who was looking for a place to rent, so she rented it to her. The friend, Maura, seems like she'll be the perfect tenant.

Thank you, Lord, for providing Brenda.

Chapter 50: The Providence Of God In Dad's Death September 28, 1974

Dad broke his shoulder on or about Nov. 8, 2011. During follow-up medical testing, we learned that his prostate cancer had metastasized into his bladder and bones. He never recovered or improved after breaking his shoulder; he died about six weeks later on Dec. 26, 2011.

I had made reservations to be in Ellwood City from November 20 until December 3. I usually only went for about a week, but this time I had decided on two weeks. I'd made these reservations before dad broke his shoulder or before I knew anything about how bad his condition was. This, of course, was the providence of God.

At the end of that visit, I did fly back to Texas on December 3 to take care of some responsibilities at home. I then returned to Ellwood less than a week later on December 9. Sandy encouraged me to get a one-way ticket, which I did. Dad continued to slowly decline; hospice, however, said he could potentially live for weeks or months because his vital signs were strong, and he showed no indication of "actively dying." I certainly wasn't hoping for dad to die, but I also had plane reservations for Africa and was scheduled to be there from January 10-22, so I wasn't sure what to do.

I didn't want to leave dad, yet hospice said he could live for a while longer. I had contacted my travel agent about refunds, changing flights, flight insurance, etc., and I was going to, during the next couple of days, contact others about fulfilling my responsibilities in Africa. I had also emailed my contacts in both the Central African Republic and Cameroon to apprise them of the situation.

Dad's death on December 26 alleviated my problems and concerns about what to do regarding the Africa trip. I know it sounds selfish to say it, but God answered my prayers for guidance through dad's death. One of my favorite verses is becoming Psalm 139:16 – "All the days ordained for me were written in your book before one of them came to be."

By the providence of God, He ordained the days for my dad in order for me to hopefully fulfill His purposes for my trip to Africa as the Executive Director of the International Association of Evangelical Chaplains. Praise God also for His faithfulness and guidance, even when walking through the valley of the shadow of death.

Chapter 51:
God's Prompting To Pray
December 27, 2011

In her own words, an email Sandy sent to Casey and Kelly:

As I am getting older, I do not always sleep really well in the early hours of the morning. I often wake up about 5:30 a.m. and then doze off and on until 7:00 a.m.

I had talked to your dad on Christmas night and heard that Grandpa was continuing to decline, and that hospice was coming the next day for an early exam, but there was nothing for either me or your dad to be overly concerned about that night. Grandpa was close to dying but it did not seem imminent, and your dad had gone back to the motel around 8:30 p.m. after having spent most of Christmas day with Grandpa. So, I had nothing in particular on my mind when I went to bed on the 25th.

However, I woke up once again in the night and expected it to be the usual 5:30 a.m. or so, but I glanced over at my clock and it was only about 1 a.m. I thought basically—"Oh man, it is the middle of the night, and I will never go back to sleep." About the same time, it came to my mind that maybe I was awakened to pray for Grandpa and your dad, so I said a quick prayer like, “Lord, please be with Rich and Dick right now.” I rolled over and went back to sleep immediately. It all took maybe a minute, and I was back to sleep. I did not even remember this or think about it again until I went to bed the next night, December 26th.

I was amazed when I woke up again last night at almost the exact same time—which is what caused me to recall the night before. The exact time I was awakened to pray was when your dad was arriving back to Katera's Kove after Grandpa died. I believe the Lord was there in a special way at that very specific time and He had called on me to pray at that time as well—from hundreds of miles away.

This might sound “strange” or “weird” to you, but my mind was crystal-clear awake for that minute of time, and I prayed as I felt led to do for that very brief minute. I have heard of others awakening in the night and feeling prompted to pray. My testimony to you is to follow through in obedience. You have no idea what God might be doing at that precise moment.

Chapter 52:
Cemetery Plots For Sale
May 2012

Mom and dad bought four grave plots at Sylvania Hills Cemetery in Rochester, Pennsylvania, many years ago—possibly even back in the 1980s. They later decided, however, that they wanted interred instead at the mausoleum at the Slippery Rock Cemetery in Ellwood City. They then added Kyle's, Sandy's and my name to the deed for the graves at Sylvania Hills. Their thought was that two of the plots were for me and two were for Kyle. It also meant five names were on the deed—their names, mine, Sandy's and Kyle's.

I wanted to sell our two plots. We were going to be in Pennsylvania for a week, so I thought this would be the time to try to do so. I put newspaper ads in the *Beaver County Times*, the *Ellwood City Ledger* and on Craig's List the week before we'd be in Ellwood. The ads in the newspapers were for two weeks.

I called Sylvania Hills three different times to see how to go about selling the plots. Last Tuesday, I went down and picked up the required paperwork that needed to be signed in the event that we found a buyer for them. It was going to be very difficult to sell them, especially if we had to do so after returning to Texas. As a matter of fact, I came back from the cemetery and told Sandy we'd probably die owning the plots because of the way the paperwork needed to be done upon finding a buyer. O ye of little faith!

I got a call early last Wednesday afternoon from a funeral director in Aliquippa. He said he was working with a family that needed a plot right away. We talked about the plot, the price, etc. He said he thought the lady would be interested and that she would call me back if she was.

She called me later that day. We met at Sylvania Hills the next morning and transferred the deed. The lady, whose 60-year-old husband had just died, was very happy with the plots. She said they were just like her husband had picked them out.

I see God's hand in this in more than one way: First of all, many plots were available at Sylvania Hills at roughly the same price; the funeral director saw my ad and called me. I had previously called a funeral director in Ellwood City to see if he could give me some guidance in selling them. His advice was "good luck."

I "just so happened" to go and get the paperwork on Tuesday. This was important because I had to get Kyle's signature. I wouldn't have been able to get the paperwork and get her signature in time to transfer the plots on Thursday morning. This was because of the timing of the lady's call to me and Kyle's work schedule. And lastly, the selling of the plots was a blessing to the lady who needed them. It was evident that she liked the location, and it eased her burden during a difficult time.

So, praise God that He also sells cemetery plots, and His timing is perfect!

Chapter 53: God, Please Turn On The Electric July 1, 2012

This was my fourth year preaching in Fairmont, West Virginia. Several "God things" happened this year that I need to write down:

For starters, there was a bad storm in West Virginia the day before we drove there from Ellwood City, Pennsylvania, where we had been visiting. More than half of the state of West Virginia's population had lost their power before we arrived. This included the Dayspring Camp and Conference Center where we stayed. This meant there was no electricity, no showers and no fans. I guess there were a couple of generators running. The electric company in West Virginia said it would be seven to 10 days before the camp had any power. The temperature was in the 90s and some of the campers were a little disheartened and discouraged before work even started.

I preached the next morning (Sunday) from Elijah 17:1-7 –"Living by the brook." The message was well-received. Monday morning, I started visiting the work sites. One of the men we talked to said that, initially, some of the people on his team wanted to drive back to Illinois when they heard there was no power and that there may be a seven-to-10-day wait for it to come back. He said all of that changed after the sermon; he told me that God used the message to speak to them and they realized they needed to be there, regardless of the conditions. Praise God!

I don't think I've ever spoken when the sermons were more timely or more well-received. God's timing was perfect. I began thinking and preparing the messages six to eight months ago, and God came through with exactly what was needed when it was needed. The camp director even said one morning, "How about telling me what you're speaking on tonight, so I'll know what is going to happen during the day."

A funny thing happened Tuesday night. One of the men had gone around and was writing down guesses from folks as to when the power would come back on; people were guessing all kinds of times throughout the week. While there was no prize or anything, it was a fun thing to do. Who knew that my guess would be the closest? I guessed it would come on at 6:45 p.m. Tuesday, and it came on at 6:53 p.m.—only eight minutes off. Folks loved that, and I had some fun with it telling them I just might be a prophet and that they really needed to listen to my sermons.

It was a wonderful, God-filled week. The folks displayed unbelievable Christian character with the temperature in the mid-to-high 90s while doing difficult construction work. God truly blessed us in the midst of difficult circumstances.

Chapter 54: Trust-Building Exercises March 2, 2014

The following is from an email Sandy sent—to our kids, I believe:

My session this week of Ann Voskamp's book is Session 4 on trust-building moments. It is exceptionally good (Chapter 8 in the book, Darcie). Anyway, there were 11 pages of "between-session" homework/activities to do afterward. One was called "Trust-Stretching Moments" and the other was "Trust-Building Moments." They asked us to recall things from our pasts and to think how God has used them to build bridges, as she calls it, and to grow our trust over the years.

So, quite randomly, I am meditating on these questions and for the trust-building moments I thought about when Casey was about 10 years old and we had just started the orthodontic work on him that lasted about five years. He appeared to have significant buckteeth, but it turned out that he actually had a very receded bottom jaw. We were told at that time that he would require jaw surgery in the future.

Long story short, Casey had enough bone/skeletal growth that his jaw came forward and he did not require the surgery. Praise the Lord for that! We were then to take that episode and tell how it helped build our faith and gave us a foundation. So, then Sarah came to my mind: Here she is at the beginning of an approximately five-year wait to see if she will need jaw surgery for her TMJ.

The situations are different, but can't the God who grew Casey's jawbone also be the God who builds up and heals Sarah's jawbone? The statement posed in the DVD states, "Hasn't God earned our trust?" It suggests that we share some of our stories with somebody younger than us. I'm 61, and you are younger, so I thought I'd share.

And that's the rest of the story, but not the end of the testimony perhaps…

Chapter 55: Not The Old Ticker September 7, 2014

For a few days I had been having a tightness/squeezing sensation in my upper-left chest; it happened twice for about two hours each. The pain or discomfort wasn't terrible, but was clearly there and not normal. This past Tuesday afternoon I called to get an appointment with my primary care manager and was able to get an appointment for the next morning.

Sandy went with me to the doctor. While in the waiting room, I had a short, 15-minute episode, including feeling clammy. After explaining to my doctor what was going on, he sent me, via ambulance, to the emergency room of Stone Oak Methodist Hospital. I arrived there, was checked out and was admitted to the hospital.

Over the next day, I had a chest X-ray, blood enzyme tests every few hours, an echocardiogram, a stress test and two 20-minute X-ray-type pictures after being injected with a radioactive dye. The bottom line is that my arteries are good with no blockages.

The issue is a mild case of cardiac myopathy—a weakening of my heart so that it doesn't pump out as much blood as it should. I am now on medication that is supposed to strengthen the muscle so it will squeeze out more blood. We have no idea how long I've had the condition; it could be something recent or could be something that has been there for a long time.

The God part is that this cardiac myopathy shouldn't cause the pressure I was feeling. So, I was checked for whatever was causing the pressure and tightness and something else was found that needed to be addressed. Praise God!

Chapter 56: Protection Overseas December 7, 2014

I attended Global Interaction 2014 in Cape Town, South Africa. While there, God clearly protected me when I was confronted by a young South African on the street, which included him jabbing me once in the chest. I turned and walked away, only to have him follow me into a fast-food restaurant and continue to yell at me in a language I did not understand. Seeing this, a large man from the Congo stepped in between us and ran the guy off.

As I was getting my food, the Congolese man came and told me that the man who had harassed me was outside and was waiting for me on the street. He said that after I received my food he would walk me to my hotel, which was about 100 yards away. He not only did so, but escorted me into the lobby and scolded the desk clerk for not taking better care of the hotel's guests.

God clearly protected me here. If the young man had had a weapon and wanted to harm me, or the Congolese man hadn't intervened, the outcome would have been different. Praise God that He intervenes, even in surprising ways!

Cape of Good Hope
South Africa
December 7, 2014

Chapter 57: I Am His June 2015

I have been having GI problems since last September. Since then, I have had a heart catheterization, a cardiac MRI, two ultrasounds, two CT scans, an endoscopy and three trips to the emergency room. I've learned that I have minor cardiac artery disease, a small hiatal hernia, gallstones and a 3.5", fluid-filled kidney cyst. After much prayer—and going back and forth regarding a decision—I put myself on travel restriction and took myself off of a trip to Uganda and Kenya. God provided Chet Arnold to go in my place.

My health and making good decisions about my health have been a matter of prayer. A few weeks ago, I was sincerely seeking the Lord and praying about it one morning during my prayer time. It wasn't in audible words, but in a way I can't explain, I sensed God saying, "I've got you" to me. There was nothing more than that—no promises of healing or anything else, just "I've got you."

I immediately had a sense of knowing I belonged to God, and regardless of what the result of my GI problems were, that I was His. What a comfort and encouragement to have that truth made real to me when I needed it. Hallelujah!

Chapter 58: Aggravations Turn Out For Our Good (Part 1) March 2016

I have a love-hate relationship with airlines. On more than one occasion, an airline has inadvertently changed my ticket and then let me know of the change after the fact. Of course, the airline is very sorry for the inconvenience. The changes have never been to my benefit—or so I thought.

This happened recently. We are currently planning to take our grandsons, Braden and Ashton, on an Alaskan cruise. Buying plane tickets into Vancouver, British Columbia, to catch the cruise ship was confusing. Because of the difficulty, I ended up buying two one-way tickets each for the four of us. Even with these tickets we didn't have as much time as we would have liked between getting off the cruise ship and our flight leaving Vancouver. Plus, we had to fly through Los Angeles—something we don't care to do.

Making a long story short and skipping a step, I got an email saying our flights had been changed. The airline had us leaving Vancouver and flying to Houston with less than an hour layover to catch a plane to San Antonio. After praying for grace, I called the airline. The lady on the phone worked things out for me. As a result, we had more time to catch the first plane. The change also had us flying through Denver instead of Los Angeles. That is also good! Our layover time is shorter, but we would still rather be in Denver—and we will still get back to San Antonio at about the same time.

Large companies, airlines being just one example, bother me because they know they are in charge and many times the consumer has little to say. One of the things I've learned is that those who "call the shots" in my life only do so because God has put them in the position to do so. I'm reminded of Pilate's authority over Jesus in John 19:10-11. "So Pilate said to him [Jesus], 'You will not speak to me? Do you not know that I have authority to release you and authority to crucify you?' Jesus answered him, 'You would have no authority over me at all unless it had been given you from above.'"

The same is true in my life, and I praise Him for it.

Chapter 59: Aggravations Turn Out For Our Good (Part 2) April 2016

During the past year we have had two situations that were aggravating and frustrating, yet that turned out to be for our good. It has just taken me until this week to realize it though. The last chapter explained the first one.

The second has to do with our insurance company. We bought insurance for both cars and our home when we moved to San Antonio in 2006. I don't remember any problems at all for the first nine years. Then, about March of 2015, I received a letter from the insurance company saying our homeowner policy was being canceled because I failed to sign one form when we purchased the policies back in 2006. I called the insurance company, as well as our local agent, to find out what was going on.

I assumed there was an error. It turns out I had not signed a piece of paper when we initially got the policy and now, nine years later, the insurance company noticed. I downloaded the proper form, signed it, mailed it to the insurance company and didn't think any more about it. A brief time later, I got a second letter saying my homeowner policy had been canceled because I hadn't signed the form. I again called the insurance company and explained I had signed it and mailed it back to them.

The lady on the phone verified that they had received it, but that didn't matter. My policies were still canceled. I called my local agent again and she said this is something this insurance company had started doing for reasons she could not explain. They seemingly inadvertently began canceling policies and only letting folks know after the fact. My insurance agent called the insurance company on my behalf and did get the policy reinstated. By then, however, I was so frustrated that I canceled it and got policies on both cars and the house with USAA instead.

Fast forward a year when we had a major hailstorm. The hailstorm was last Tuesday evening as we drove home from a Spurs game. I called USAA the next morning to file claims on my house and car; an insurance estimator came two days later to look at my roof. A few days later, USAA cut a check to replace my roof. I can't believe how prompt the service was—I had a check for a new roof, minus my deductible, within a week of the hailstorm. I can't imagine going through the claim process with the insurance company I had at first. That company canceled me because of an unsigned paper nine years before. Can you imagine trying to get them to handle and pay a claim now?

Although the initial hassle with the first insurance company was aggravating and frustrating, God worked it out for our welfare a year later when we actually had to file a claim. We never even knew there was a problem, but God knew, and He took care of it for us.

Chapter 60: Should I Get On The Plane? April 6, 2017

I returned a few days ago from a quick trip to Cote d'Ivoire. I left home on a Friday and got back home the next Thursday evening. It is typical that when I travel overseas, especially to Africa, I have stomach issues. I attribute them to traveling long distances, trying new foods, eating at odd times or a combination of all of these. Whatever the reason, there is typically a bad day or two of not feeling 100 percent during the trip. I am usually at my destination long enough to deal with it and get over whatever the problem is, but not this time; I was only there for four days.

When I boarded the plane in Abidjan, Cote d'Ivoire, for Paris, where I changed planes to return home, my stomach wasn't feeling great. I had eaten a delicious rabbit stew a few hours before going to the Abidjan airport, and now was thinking that this probably hadn't been a good idea. Although I did not feel terrible, I didn't eat much on the overnight flight from Abidjan to Paris.

We landed in Paris, and as I stood in the aisle waiting to exit the plane, I could feel my heart start to race. I was concerned about why this was happening. I had quite a lengthy walk to my gate and had to go through security again. Maybe it really wasn't, but my heart seemed like it was racing even faster as I navigated the airport to my next flight.

After finding my gate, I used the nearby restroom and felt better . . . for a few minutes. After another trip to the restroom, another few minutes of feeling OK. As my heart continued to race and the intestinal discomfort returned again, I began getting worried and scared. I wasn't even sure if I should board the flight.

I certainly didn't want to not take the flight and end up at an emergency room in Paris. But, not knowing what was going on physically, I also didn't want to get on the plane for a flight of more than nine hours. I took Pepto-Bismol a couple of times, but it didn't seem to help. I tried deep breathing and telling myself to relax, but there was nothing I could do to slow my heart rate down—it felt like it wanted to jump out of my chest.

Finally, after one more trip to the restroom, I began feeling like my stomach had improved somewhat and maybe my heart had slowed down a little. I still wasn't sure what to do; I typically like to board the plane as soon as I can. This time, however, I just waited and let a lot of people board in front of me. This gave me time to pray that I would make a good decision about taking the flight.

As I prayed, I remember thinking that God is sovereign, and He would providentially guide my decision. I knew I could get on the plane and, if things got worse, I could get off the plane again if they hadn't closed the doors yet. With that thought in mind, I got on the plane. I slowly began to feel better, and my heart slowly stopped racing. Within an hour or so I was back to normal.

The worst part of this episode had lasted 75 to 90 minutes. I can clearly and easily see God's hand in all of this. He allowed me to get sick when I was in an airport rather than on the plane. He also providentially guided my decision to get on the plane when I really wasn't sure what to do. Praise God for His providence.

Chapter 61: Wasps November 2017

I am in Kigali, Rwanda, for a week with Trinity Center for World Mission. Our team is teaching pastors and church leaders how to interpret the Bible. We are living, working and eating at the African Leadership and Reconciliation Ministries (ALARM) compound.

Last night, for the first time, I had some large insects that looked like wasps flying around my room. They were buzzing near the ceiling light like flying insects often do. Being severely allergic to wasp stings, I was quite concerned—I'd been stung by wasps a few months ago and it sent me to the emergency room.

I couldn't try to kill them since the ceiling was 10-12 feet high. The only thing I knew to do was to pray. I lifted my hands up toward the light and asked God to blow the insects away like He did the locusts in Exodus 10.

It was only a minute or two when one of them flew into the bathroom where the light was also on. The insect was on the sink and for some reason it didn't move; I killed it with a flip-flop. My approach then became turning the light off in the bedroom and leaving the light on in the bathroom, hoping to draw them into the bathroom. One by one, over a period of about fifteen minutes, six more flew into the bathroom and I killed them. No more flying insects!

Although I found out the next day that they were not wasps and did not sting, I didn't know that at the time and clearly see this as a direct answer to prayer—not only my prayer, but also for all those praying for me back home.

Chapter 62: How Beautiful Are The Feet December 1, 2017

I can easily get tears in my eyes when I think about the following testimony:

I am sitting right now in the Amsterdam airport. I left Kasese, Uganda, early yesterday morning after being in Rwanda and Uganda sharing the Gospel and teaching discipleship classes with Trinity Center for World Mission. I was playing Christian music on my iPhone as I was getting dressed to leave Kasese.

Just as I sat down on the edge of the bed to put my socks on, the song that began playing was John Michael Talbot's "Our God Reigns." The song starts out with these words, "How lovely on the mountains are the feet of him who brings good news." It is from Isaiah 52:7, which says, "How beautiful upon the mountains are the feet of him who brings good news, who publishes peace, who brings good news of happiness, who publishes salvation, who says to Zion, 'Your God reigns.'"

I heard the words of the song, looked at my still-sockless feet, and almost couldn't believe what I was hearing. Since God is sovereign and there are no such things as coincidences or chance, what a wonderful and gracious confirmation from God that I was doing what He wanted me to do and was exactly where He wanted me to be. What comfort and joy!

Teaching in Kasese, Uganda.

Chapter 63: God In The Small Stuff January 2019

Last Sunday evening was my first night of teaching a class on hermeneutics at University Baptist Church. Although I got several positive comments after the class, I didn't feel like it went that well. I woke up yesterday morning (Monday) and was kind of bummed about it. After my morning prayer and Bible reading, I looked for my copy of the book that I'm teaching from, "Knowing Scripture" by R.C. Sproul, but I couldn't find it. Not being able to find my own textbook for the class I'm teaching would obviously be a problem.

After looking for about 10 minutes, I got Sandy's copy of the book and started using it to prepare for the next week. About 15 minutes later, I walked into my bedroom to get something and prayed silently along the way, "Lord, please help me find that book." Within seconds, I had the thought to look in a divider that I keep folders in—maybe the book had slipped down where I couldn't see it. Sure enough, there it was. I was very glad to have the book back; more importantly, however, was my amazement at God's care over the little things.

God showed me this again later in the day. I had put some Motrin in my pocket to take later, but all the pills weren't there when the time came to take them. I wondered if I dropped one. After tracing my steps, however, I couldn't find it. As I went into the family room to read, I had a thought: "I wonder if I dropped it, and it went under the couch." That is exactly what happened—there was my Motrin.

Those kinds of experiences are not daily occurrences for me. When they happen, though, they are signs of God's love and care that point me to Him in thanksgiving and praise.

Chapter 64: God's Word Accomplishes His Purposes July 2019

I returned a few days ago from a week of preaching at Dayspring Camp and Conference Center in Fairmont, West Virginia. God gave me a special blessing the night before camp even started. A 16-year-old girl (Jeannie) came to me and said she wanted me to know that she had become a Christian because of one of my sermons two years ago. I asked her what I'd preached on, and she told me it was a sermon on Job. She said that she usually never paid very much attention to the preacher, but decided she would listen this week out of respect for me.

That year I had started my series of sermons on Job by talking about everything God allowed to be taken from him. As she listened, she began thinking about how good her life was and how God could take everything from her. Thinking about that made her realize she needed to get serious about God. She said by the end of the week she had realized that she'd become a Christian. The interesting thing is that I didn't even present the Gospel in that sermon—God did it all!

A few days later, I saw a young lady (Meghan) in her mid-to-late twenties that I hadn't seen before. She was sitting under the pavilion with her little baby. I went up and introduced myself to her. She said she and her husband lived in Columbus, Ohio, and had come over for a few days to see if they could help out at the camp. She said she knew who I was, that I was the speaker and what I was preaching on.

She then said that she was in camp 10 years ago and still remembered something I'd preached back then. She told me that I said we have to ask ourselves three questions if we are going to say something about another person. The three questions are: Is it true? Is it kind? Is it needful? I couldn't believe it. I asked how long ago that was and she said in 2009, when she was a smart aleck teenager (her words).

Saturday morning, we were saying our goodbyes before we left camp, and Ben Cooper, who works part-time for the camp, told me how meaningful the sermon the night before had been for him. I had spoken on the Fourth Commandment. Ben told me that I'd said things that not only had he never heard before, but that he could use in his ministry counseling addicts. How encouraging!

As I considered these three experiences I thought about the power of the Word of God. He had used His Word for evangelism (Jeannie), for discipleship (Meghan) and to equip the saints for ministry (Ben). I couldn't help but think of Isaiah 55:11, which says, "so shall my word be that goes out from my mouth; it shall not return to me empty, but it shall accomplish that which I purpose, and shall succeed in the thing for which I sent it."

When preaching, I don't need an agenda, fancy words or to be manipulative—I just need to be faithful in proclaiming God's Word.

Preaching at Dayspring Camp and Conference Center in Fairmont, WV.

Chapter 65: Thankful On The Maui Lanai November 2019

Sandy and I recently stayed a week on Maui in a third-floor Airbnb condo before heading to Oahu for two weeks. The condo had a small, but nice, lanai where we would sit, eat our breakfast or supper and look at the ocean. The night before we were to leave Maui, we went out on the lanai and ate our supper there. Without thinking about it, I pulled the sliding glass door closed behind me. No problem so far, except I didn't know that the door was in the locked position.

We enjoyed our supper and then tried to get back inside but couldn't. It was then we realized the sliding glass door was locked from the inside. We were stuck there on the lanai for 45 minutes to an hour before we could get back into the condo. There were a couple of providential events that allowed us to get back in.

The first was that there was a man sitting by the pool below us—remember, we were on the third floor. Sandy got his attention and told him our predicament. As well as we can remember, that was the first time during our week-long stay that someone had been sitting at the pool in the evening and close enough to hear her calling. God's timing of having him there was perfect!

The second thing is that I had my cell phone out on the lanai with me. I didn't always, but that night I did. The fact that I had my phone with me was no doubt a result of an unrealized prompting of the Holy Spirit to take it with me.

After establishing phone contact with the man by the pool, he went to the office, took a picture of the sign that had the telephone number of the assistant manager of the condo complex on it and sent it to me. With that number, after a few calls and texts, help came within the hour when the assistant manager arrived and used his master key to get into our condo and open the sliding glass door for us.

Being on the third floor meant we couldn't just climb over the railing. I am not sure what we would have done if I hadn't "just so happened" to have my cell phone with me or if the man by the pool hadn't been there. Praise God!

Chapter 66: Physical Problems (Yet Again) November 2019

God's intervention, as described below, took place within 36 hours of the previous one, "Thankful On The Maui Lanai."

We left Maui, and after a short flight to Honolulu, we got to the Hale Koa Hotel with no problems. While I had been having some back issues in Maui, it was nothing that hindered our plans there. However, I was awakened in the middle of the night with unbelievable pain the first night we were at the Hale Koa.

It went from my back down into my left hip, continued to my thigh and into my knee; I had never had that kind of pain before. It was at least an eight on a scale of 1 to 10. There was no way to get comfortable or to relieve the pain. I generally try not to take any pain meds if possible, but did get up and take a strong pain medicine and a muscle relaxer.

I woke Sandy up with all my squirming trying to relieve the pain. I couldn't lay down, sit, walk, kneel, crouch or do pretty much anything else without terrible pain. That was also the day we were to pick up the rental car, and, by the grace of God, I improved enough that we could get the rental car. I spent most of the next two days in the hotel not doing any more than I had to while Sandy washed all our clothes.

Now, almost two weeks later, I am still not fully back to normal. I'm taking 800 mg of Motrin three times a day and some Robaxin at least once a day. My left thigh feels kind of numb and has for several days.

Not only do I praise God that I've been able to function relatively well, but I also praise God for His timing in this. Had it occurred 24 hours before, I would not have been able to fly to Oahu. That would have been a major headache, as all the reservations on Oahu would have needed to be adjusted. We also had to leave our Airbnb condo in Maui and would have needed to find other accommodations until I could travel to Honolulu. Once more—His timing is perfect, even to the smallest detail.

Chapter 67:
A Leaky Shower
January 2020

Like so many of the things I've written here, this one also has to do with the providence of God. It all began a few weeks ago when our handyman, Bill, was hanging a shed door for me. I asked him if he'd also look at some paint that was peeling on my master bathroom wall because I thought the drywall might need to be replaced. He looked at it, peeled a little paint back and said he thought we might have mold. He said there could be a small leak somewhere and that I should call my insurance company because mold remediation can be costly. I called USAA that afternoon; the lady I talked to wasn't encouraging about any damage being covered.

Bill had told me that the mold-remediation companies work with plumbers and other contractors to do everything that needs to be done. He said they'd find the leak, fix it, take care of the mold and give me a certificate saying the house was mold-free. I began researching mold-remediation companies and called one. A receptionist took my message and said someone would call me back. A week later, and after a second phone to call to them, the company hadn't returned my call.

In hindsight, I see this as the providence of God; if the company had called me back, I never would have done the next thing, which proved to be important. I physically drove to a place called Rainbow International where I talked to Tammy, the desk clerk. In the providence of God, her last job had been working at my insurance company in the property claim department—the same folks I'd called a week earlier and didn't get any encouragement to file the claim. Tammy said there was a good chance it would be covered by my insurance and that I should call USAA back and speak to another representative.

I did so that afternoon and told them I wanted to formally file the claim. This USAA rep (Joe) told me the first thing to do was to get a plumber to look at it and diagnose the problem. I did that. He couldn't find the leak without doing several expensive tests.

Long story short—a day or so later I got a call from a USAA field adjuster who scheduled some plumbers to find the leak. Again, in the providence of God, she was able to come while they were here. She said this rarely happened, and it proved to be a blessing, as she could talk to the plumbers about the leak problem rather than just read each other's reports.

USAA paid for the plumbers, who did find the leak after running numerous tests. The USAA field adjuster was here when they found the leak and immediately started the ball rolling to get things fixed. Other than my deductible and fixing the leak behind the wall, USAA paid for everything else. This included tearing everything apart, new tile in the whole bathroom, a new shower enclosure, fixing and painting all the drywall, etc. She also said we did not have any mold issues and that she would make sure this was included in her report.

I see God's hand written all over this. The mold-remediation company I first contacted didn't call me back after a week; if it had done so, I would have had them come and not pursued calling USAA again because of what I'd been told by the USAA representative the first time I called. Tammy's last job was at USAA in the property claim department; it was because of her encouragement that I called USAA back to speak to another representative. And the USAA field adjuster was here when the plumbers found the leak. These are not coincidences—they are examples of a sovereign God taking care of His children. Hallelujah!

Chapter 68: Keeper Of The Heart January 2020

Sandy started having some serious back issues last month—serious enough that she took some Percocet, which really sent her for a loop with dizziness and not feeling well. It was severe enough that she even went to the doctor. While her blood pressure is always high at the doctor's office, it was higher than usual for this appointment. We attribute this to the fact that she was in pain. The doctor gave her a prescription for a muscle relaxant that made her really tired.

Because her blood pressure had been so high, and the doctor wanted to see her again about it, we began measuring and documenting it at home. A couple of times when on the muscle relaxant her blood pressure seemingly went the other direction and was so low that we didn't think our blood pressure machine was accurate. That being the case, I went out and bought another one.

This new one was the same kind, only it has a few more features—like an indicator when it detects an irregular heartbeat. Sure enough, it showed that she not only had an irregular heartbeat occasionally, but that her pulse was abnormally low occasionally too. Both low readings usually showed up at the same time. Sandy went back to the doctor to go over the results of taking it at home. He did an EKG, which was "borderline" because of a possible enlarged atrium. She also had a chemical stress test, and, thankfully, it was normal. The next step is a cardiology appointment in a couple of weeks. In hindsight, we are now quite sure the old blood pressure machine was OK because the new one also registered some low blood pressure readings.

We see God's hand in this in a couple of ways. The first is that while going to the doctor initially for back pain, issues were discovered that are leading to more testing for a possible heart problem. Also, this prompted me to go out and buy another blood pressure machine that showed the irregular heartbeat, which was not a capability of the older machine. The irregular heartbeat reading is what got the ball rolling to see a cardiologist and determine if Sandy has any heart problems. Truly, He is a God of the heart . . . in more ways than one!

Chapter 69: Painting Of Shiloh December 25, 2020

Very sadly for us, Shiloh, our Cocker Spaniel, died Dec. 27, 2020, about three and a half weeks ago. It was a very sad time, and the grief was (and still is to some degree) very real. Sandy and I are the only ones who know just how special she was—a true gift from God.

She went into the hospital on December 23. Christmas rolled around and it wasn't the same, with her in the hospital and us not knowing if she would make it or not. Casey and Darcie got a painting of Shiloh for me for Christmas. I began crying as soon as I saw what it was, even before getting it totally unwrapped. I showed it to Sandy, and she did the same. It is an excellent painting with an unbelievable resemblance to Shiloh.

Our son Casey had the painting done by Kelly Chang, a man he had done some work with. Casey asked Kelly to paint it months ago—long before we even knew Shiloh was sick. After seeing how good the painting was, Sandy wanted to thank Kelly for it. She asked Casey to forward the following email to him:

"Dear Mr. Kelly Chang,

I apologize that it has taken us so very long to write to you concerning Shiloh's painting. Casey already told us that you know Shiloh died two days after Christmas. She was already in the vet hospital on Christmas Day, which is when we opened your painting present from Casey and Darcie.

The painting initially was very hard for us to look at since it reminded us so much of the little girl we were losing. Casey said you are an animal lover, so you can understand our grief. She was only 8 1/2 years old when she died.

We were able to hang her picture yesterday in the room she loved the most—the TV room, where she spent so much of her time looking out the window from the couch and being with my husband while he watched TV at night. It looks perfect in that room.

I also wanted to mention how very much it looks like Shiloh. You captured her personality in the painting so well. She was a very sweet and docile pet and was so willing to please us at every turn. She had been sick since birth and required lots of doctoring and meds, but she never fought us or "complained" about her hard life. She was a happy and very well-loved pet.

We do hope that you caught a sense of her preciousness as you painted her. We wish you could have met her. The framing is very beautiful too, and it was very special to have your photo taped on the back of the painting.

We did want to tell you that Shiloh was a rescue pet. We got her from a hoarding situation in Dallas and we fell in love with her the minute we met her. As a rescue, the original owner had never gotten any of the puppies' tails docked, and we so loved her tail. We are so glad that it is included prominently in the painting. It was always wagging to tell us she was happy and content.

I have gone on too long here, but I did not want to only thank you for the time you spent getting to know Shiloh and painting her so well, but I wanted you to know more about our Shiloh too. We miss her so much.

I have sent a photo of your painting to other family members and friends, and they all raved about how good it is. Please accept our heartfelt thank you for making such a treasured remembrance of Shiloh for us.

We wish you and your family well.

Blessings,

Sandy and Rich Young

Mr. Chang sent Casey the following email back:

Good morning, Mr. Young,

Happy New Year. Let me express my sincere condolences to you and to your parents with the passing of Shiloh. I don't have the words to describe the tremendous loss your parents are feeling. The email your parents shared with me was heartfelt, warm, loving and sincere. I can hear in their voices how much they loved her and how this special dog impacted their day-to-day lives. It was very emotional reading this letter.

I consider myself just an ordinary recreational painter. When you asked me to paint Shiloh for your parents, I was honored and scared. I knew how special this dog was to your father and mother and did not want to disappoint them. I was truly happy to hear they approved of the painting.

This past Tuesday I had a heart attack. I am doing just fine and recovering. I wanted to share this with you because the day I came home from the hospital this is the email I opened first.

Honestly, I read this email from your parents about 10 times. I was really down on myself. Something like a heart attack changes a person, but after reading your parents' email something just energized me emotionally. I was crying and smiling at the same time. Your parents' letter saved me. I have a whole new perspective about my life and what I need to do going forward. I will always treasure this letter. Please send my deepest condolences and gratitude to your parents.

Chapter 70: The Coveted Coronavirus Vaccines January 2021

It has now been about 10 months since COVID-19 began sweeping across the country and the world. Life changed when that happened last March. God willing, things are now taking a turn to bring the coronavirus somewhat under control. Of course, vaccines are a huge part of that, and about five weeks ago vaccinations started becoming available for people in San Antonio; Americans are supposed to get two shots that are 28 days apart.

The process began by giving the vaccines to those who are most vulnerable. Frontline healthcare workers were first, I think; they were followed by first responders, then the elderly and those with underlying health conditions. About two week's ago, they got to our age group—those over 65. Being in the correct age group, however, certainly did not guarantee getting the first shot though, since appointments to get the vaccine were few and far between.

San Antonio was getting in about 9,000 doses a week. Remembering that San Antonio has a population of about 1.5 million, with about 60 percent of them being more than 65 years old, the odds of getting one was very small. I tried to get an appointment the first week by calling the phone number we were given on television; I tried well over 100 times and could get nothing but a busy signal. That particular week, there were supposedly 5.6 million telephone calls with folks trying to get one of the 9,000 doses.

The next week came, and I tried again after Bible study on Saturday morning. Although I initially planned on only trying 100 times, for reasons unknown to me, I dialed once more and I got through on my 101st try. Our appointment was for Monday morning, about 48 hours from when I got through. We have talked to others who have tried literally thousands of times to get through on the phone and couldn't; we had prayed and asked God to not only help us get through, but also to have us get through when He wanted us to have the shot. I'm sure countless others said a similar prayer. Why He answered our prayers so quickly and not others is known only to Him. We know He did get my call answered and we are very thankful. Hallelujah!

We did get the first dose of the vaccine yesterday with almost no side effects at all—only very minor pain in my arm this morning. We already have our appointments for the second shot in four weeks. The television news said last night that in the last eight days there have been eight million phone calls trying to get one of the 9,000 doses. We don't know why God treated us so well, but He did, and we praise Him.

Chapter 71: Ice Storm And Providence Of God February 2021

Casey came to visit last week; it was a working visit. He worked in my office, where he could be by himself and be online. He did take one day off and quit early a couple of afternoons so we could do something with him. In hindsight, we now see how providential the timing of his visit was.

Before getting to that, however, I need to mention the storm that began the day after he left. He flew home on a Saturday. Had he waited until Sunday, he would not have made it out due to the weather and canceled flights. Of course, none of us knew about the bad storm headed our way when he bought his ticket weeks earlier. The storm was the worst in decades with temps down into the single digits, snow, power lost for more than 300,000 people in San Antonio, no water for thousands of folks, roads totally shut down, fire hydrants freezing and hospitals needing to move patients to other hospitals because they had no electricity. Things here were really, really bad!

While Casey was here, we thought we were having problems with our security system and our diagnosis was that we needed a new battery. So, I went out and bought another one, but it turned out that this was not the case. As a result, I had an extra battery.

A week later, in the middle of the storm with no power, our security system started beeping again, but in a different way. This time it was flashing, "New battery needed." And, due to buying it the week before, I already had one and installed it in about 30 seconds. I would not have been able to go and buy another one during the storm, so what a blessing to already have it here.

Also, if the storm had come a week earlier—or Casey had come a week later—he would not have been able to work from here because we lost the Internet when we lost our power. Another providential blessing that he came the week he did. God's timing is always perfect!

Chapter 72: Stop This Terrible Spinning! June 11, 2021

I woke up yesterday morning with vertigo. My alarm went off at 4:00 a.m., as it usually does, and I promptly knocked it off the chair beside my bed without getting it turned off. Instinctively almost, I reached out to get it on the floor. While trying to find it without getting out of bed, I even knocked over the kitchen chair it had been resting on. I finally found it, turned it off and laid back on the bed for a minute.

While lying there, I noticed that the blue light on my printer, indicating it was turned on, didn't look right—it looked like there were either two lights where there should have been only one or one that was much bigger than it should have been. At first, I attributed this to not having my glasses on. I then realized my head was spinning like crazy and I began to not feel well.

Within a few minutes, I felt nauseated and made the first of four trips to the restroom in the next two hours. Beside the fact that I felt lousy, it was also on my mind that I was supposed to teach Bible study for a friend who was on vacation. The Bible study began at 6:30 a.m. and I needed to leave at about 6:00 a.m., giving me less than two hours to feel better and leave.

For those two hours, I was up and down trying to find a position that would relieve the spinning in my head. This included brushing my teeth while lying on the bathroom floor. The only position that seemed to minimize the spinning was to have my shoulders back and my head facing straight ahead without looking either to the right or the left. It was best for me to either sit or stand like that, but lying down was OK too. I also sweat badly for quite a while. I was not 100 percent better by 6:00 p.m., but good enough to drive to Bible study and teach.

I felt strongly that God wanted me to lead the study—I felt equally strongly that Satan did not. My subject was, "What is the Gospel?" To explain the Gospel, I was going to make a contrast between the non-Christian's stand before God and the Christian's stand before God on Judgment Day. As I was teaching it, and reflecting on it afterwards, I am confident those who were in attendance were helped by this. Based on the comments and questions I received, there is a good probability that at least one of the men present was not a Christian. Even a couple of guys there who I know to be Christians seemed to be listening particularly intently as I spoke.

All of that said, I praise God that He helped me feel well enough to teach the class and share the Gospel with seven other men. The Gospel is the power of God for salvation. Lord, may it be true in at least one life yesterday.

Chapter 73: Apparently, I've Had A Stroke June 20, 2021

This is a follow-up to the previous story, "Please Stop This Terrible Spinning!" The last week has been a whirlwind. I was supposed to fly to Pittsburgh last Monday morning, spend four days there, drive to West Virginia to preach for a week in Fairmont and then immediately fly home a few days before Sandy's scheduled surgery.

Last Sunday afternoon, the day before flying, I had an episode of feeling funny and having blurry vision for about 15 minutes. The rest of the day consisted of several trips to the restroom. Monday morning, I woke up at 2:00 a.m. and was supposed to leave at about 3:30 a.m. for the airport. Still not feeling well, I woke Sandy up at 3:10 a.m. and told her she needed to take me to the emergency room.

We went to the ER, and I had a five-to-six-hour stay. During that time, they did lab work, an EKG and a CT scan. The doctor came in eventually and told us that, due to computer problems, the radiology department was not able to view the CT scan as clearly as it would like to. From what they could see, however, it didn't seem to show any problems. Assuming the CT scan was good, the doctor discharged me, and we went home—that was late Monday morning. I immediately called my point of contact in West Virginia and told him I would not be able to make the trip to preach the next week.

We were at home Wednesday evening when I received a call from the ER doctor who had discharged me just two days earlier. She said the computers were now working, the radiologist had read my CT scan and it showed that at some point in my past I had had a stroke. I mentioned to her that I had an episode of blurry vision earlier that day, and she told me I needed to go to the ER right away to see if there was any stroke activity right then.

We took off for the ER, I was examined and was admitted to the hospital to get an MRI of my head. Every time someone mentioned it to me, I told them I needed a sedative and that a small Xanax or Ativan wasn't enough—this was (and is still) important to me because of my claustrophobia. I had been claustrophobic while getting an MRI in the past, and they were not able to get good pictures as a result because of me moving around too much. This time, they gave me a stronger sedative before the MRI, and it went fine.

Part of the discussion in the ER was with two different doctors at two separate times about whether or not I wanted to be resuscitated or intubated if I crashed. I told them I did not want either, so they put DNR (Do Not Resuscitate) and DNI (Do Not Intubate) on my chart.

Bottom line: I was given 5 mg of valium for the MRI, and it went very well—no issues of claustrophobia at all. The MRI verified a previous stroke "months to years in the past." No other problems or areas of concern were found and I was not having any kind of acute episode.

We see God's Hand in all of this. By His providence, I made the right decision to not fly to Pittsburgh and travel to West Virginia; I would not have wanted the vertigo, light-headedness or blurred vision to happen when I was not at home. As a result of not traveling the day I was supposed to, or even later in the week, I was at home when the doctor called me to go back to the ER because of the misread CT scan; had I received that call in either Pennsylvania or West Virginia, I'm not sure what I would have done. As a result of knowing I've had a Lacuna Stroke in the past, they've adjusted my medications to hopefully prevent another stroke in the future. And lastly, the doctors were all very receptive to my need for a sedative during the MRI and the procedure could not have gone better.

These are just the examples I can think of as I write this. There are likely other incidents that I'm not recalling and may even be areas where God intervened that I'm not even aware of. For all these, whether recognized or not, we praise God for orchestrating all of the details and for taking care of me.

When I stop to reflect on what could have been, I am very thankful for God's gracious hand on my life by protecting me from serious consequences. And, the trip to the ER and hospital led to other tests, which brought attention to other issues that needed to be followed up on.

Chapter 74: A New Family Member June 20, 2021

Shiloh, the sweetest dog in the world, died last December 27. We were heartbroken and can still get choked up if we think about her and what a wonderful dog she was—there will never be another one like her for us. Thankfully, the grief is slowly lessening, and we decided about a month ago that we're ready for another pet.

I began looking at rescue places online, and we filled out a couple of applications so we would be waiting in the wings with an approved application when the right dog came along. We were looking for a small, female puppy. There were options on a couple of different websites, but nothing we considered a real possibility for us. One rescue place didn't approve our application because it only placed puppies in a home if there were other dogs. We have also run across a couple of places that would only adopt to people less than sixty years old. Obviously, not us!

I mentioned to my friend Bill at Bible Study that we were looking for puppy. He said he and his family had fostered a puppy for a rescue group and then decided to adopt it. He made an inquiry for us and gave me the name of the rescue group: It was God's Dogs Rescue. Providentially, I had just seen their website for the first time the night before.

I filled out an application. Two weeks later I still hadn't heard anything, so I emailed again. Then things began to happen immediately. A lady named Lorraine was our adoption counselor. She referred me to a lady I'll call Gloria, who called me the next morning to tell me about the dogs she was fostering.

One was bigger than we wanted (more than 30 pounds) and the other was smaller than we wanted (less than 10 pounds). After explaining this to her, she told me about a foster mom named Flo who had puppies available that were not even in the God's Dogs Rescue system or on their website yet. Flo called me the next day. We talked about her puppies, and she sent me pictures of their mother and who they think the dad is. Mom is a miniature schnauzer mix; dad was a little guy traveling through town. I have pictures of both and also had a chance to meet the puppies' mom—her name is Rosie.

Because the pups had not been put on the website yet, we had our pick of the litter. Sandy chose Piper (who Flo had named Button because she was cute as a button) while looking at Flo's Facebook Live video. I was on the phone with Flo while we watched the puppies on Facebook Live.

Doing it that way was perfect, since Flo could tell us about each of the puppies as we watched them. We picked Piper up yesterday and we know our lives are getting ready to change. She will be our fourth puppy, and we are looking forward to raising another one. We see God's hand present in Bill mentioning to me about his experiences with fostering and adopting, in Gloria mentioning to me about Flo and her puppies, and in Flo being such a great foster mom and being so easy to work with.

We got Shiloh from a rescue place in Dallas. Before doing so, we prayed frequently that God would give us the perfect dog just for us. He did that with Shiloh, and we are thankful for the time we had with her and for the love that flowed both ways. We have prayed the same thing about Piper. We praise God that He has given her to us, for however long it may be . . . and we're hoping it is a long time!

Chapter 75: Tabletalk, Emails And The Providence Of God August 7, 2021

Below are two emails from Sandy. The first one she sent out this morning; the second she sent a few hours later. Both were sent to our family as well as to a couple of her closest friends.

Email No. 1:

"I don't usually preach to the choir, but I read this a few weeks ago and it comes to mind almost daily. I think about it when somebody says something that reminds me to stop reacting to life from my feelings or "how I feel about something." That will usually lead me astray.

I was reading an article in the June 2021 *Tabletalk* magazine called 'A Woman's Identity In Christ' by Susan Smith Bennett. She includes a quote in it from Martin Lloyd-Jones that simply says: "Stop listening to ourselves and start speaking to ourselves."

It sounds so simple-minded, and yet it really is quite deep. What is running through my brain during the day? What do I hear when something happens? How do I respond to life in general? Do I react out of my feelings (be it fear or arrogance or guilt or past hurts or self-reliance) *or* do I tell myself what God says in His Word? There are so many promises of God in Scripture and instructions on how to deal with life. So how do I respond?

If you do spend some time to think about this, I think your mindset will change. What am I thinking and feeling when something happens and how does it compare to what God has said about it? It really is introspective.

Anyway, I think it is something to share. I think if I had a group right now, I would be discussing it with them. I find so many women who fall into this trap—over and over again—and I'm sure men do too.

The paragraph in the magazine ends with this, 'We must speak truth to ourselves.'

Maybe this will be meaningful to you too.

Blessings,

Sandy"

<u>Email No. 2:</u>

"Some of you may not have even read this original note (above) yet, and here I am commenting on it already. That is because God apparently does NOT waste time. If you read this well, you will note that I said, 'If I had a group right now, I would be discussing it with them.'

Less than one hour after sending it, I got a note from my friend Ruth in Uganda. I met her and her husband David in Carlisle, Pennsylvania, in 2009 at one of our Chaplain Interactions. We have kept in touch over the years and keep up with notes from time to time. After Ginny Cole and I held our women's ministry class at Carlisle, she went back to Uganda and started a thriving wives group that continues to meet monthly. They do wonderful service projects together and look after each other. Plus, she oversees their Bible studies.

Anyway, I got an email from her this morning asking me to please speak to her Zoom group. They are meeting this way now since Uganda has closed down again due to COVID. She told me that Ginny spoke to the group last month. Of course, I was going to immediately write back and tell Ruth 'No' because that is how I roll on things like this. Instead, I wrote to Ginny to ask her questions about her Zoom session with the group, and she was very encouraging to me and told me that I should do it.

So, I have not written back to Ruth yet, but could this be the group I thought I needed to share my thoughts about facts over feelings when listening to God? How can it not be, right? Just way too coincidental for me. I will write back to Ruth and get more details at least. I am praying that I am not a 'weenie' at this point :-) The fact that I even sent that out this morning is way out of the norm for me, and then for Ruth to write so soon afterwards—way to go, God!"

Sandy did eventually say yes to Ruth's request, and they began emailing back and forth about the details. When a week went by without Sandy hearing from Ruth we started wondering what had happened. I then received an email from a mutual friend saying Ruth had died unexpectantly after a short hospitalization. We do not know why, but she is now with the Lord.

Chapter 76: Kelly's Job (written by him) April 2022

When I started writing these, one of the primary purposes was that my children and grandchildren would come to know Jesus Christ in a personal way. I still, with all of my heart, want them to know the God of their father. Below is a Facebook post that Kelly put up this morning. I think his post shows that God is indeed answering my prayer. Here is what he wrote:

"Forgive me if this comes off as braggy—it is intended to be 'Praise God from whom all blessings flow-y.' Back in 2014, when *American Rifleman* hired me as an associate editor, I immediately knew that I had landed my dream job and that the only career aspiration left for me was to kick enough butt here that it hopefully convinced them to let me stay forever. Since that time, my pie-in-the-sky hopes were that I could one day, far in the distant future, rise through the ranks to the point that I was number two at the magazine with the title of senior executive editor. And I'm talking decades down the road.

Well, in one of the more surreal landmarks to ever occur in my life, today marks one year since both of those things happened—and I'm still young enough to have all of my own teeth! It's even more absurd when I consider that I had no previous experience in this industry when I was hired, and after more than seven years at the magazine I now understand full-well how extremely rarely that occurs. I am a level of blessed that is difficult to process at times, and this is one of those times—and that's not even touching on the undeserved spiritual justification or the awesome wife."

Chapter 77: The Providence Of God And A Dead Battery May 5, 2023

I went to a coin club meeting last night on San Pedro Avenue, about 12 or 13 miles from home. After the meeting, I got in the car to come home and tried starting it, but to no avail; the battery was dead. I tried a couple more times, and the result was the same—click, click, click. It wouldn't start.

I sat there for a few seconds trying to decide if I should call AAA or Sandy first. Just then, a young lady who just so happened to be parked next to me got my attention and asked me if I needed a jump. She had jumper cables in her hands like I'd never seen before; it was a small box, even smaller than a loaf of bread. It had two cables coming out of it, one with a red clamp and one with a black clamp.

I put them on my battery and the car started right up. The young lady's name was Betsy, and she's also a member of the coin club, although we'd never met. From the time I walked out of the meeting to when I was pulling out of the parking lot with a jumped car was probably not much more than five minutes.

I see God's hand in this in more ways than one. Betsy "just so happened" to be parked next to me in the parking lot. She walked up to her car at the exact time I was trying to get mine started; a few minutes earlier or a few minutes later and she would not have known my quandary. I am writing this the next day, and I had an appointment this morning for a CT scan that I left for at about 7 a.m.—had the car battery been dead this morning instead of last night, I may have had trouble getting to the appointment.

I also looked through my paperwork and found that the battery was still under warranty, so I got it replaced for free. And lastly, we will drive the car to the airport in a few days and leave it in the parking garage for a week. There is a good chance that, had the battery not died last night, we would have returned home after a week away and had a dead battery in the parking garage of the airport. We are very thankful for God's providential care and His faithfulness in caring for us in so many ways during this ordeal.

Chapter 78: God's Umbrella July 2023

I was at IMPACT West Virginia in Fairmont last week; I think it was my 11th year preaching there. IMPACT West Virginia is a ministry in which church teams come to Fairmont for a week to carry out different projects. Last week we had teams doing different types of work on six different houses—this includes remodeling a bathroom, putting a new floor on a front porch, installing a drop ceiling in a kitchen, putting in a new sidewalk and painting a two-story house. Other teams conducted Vacation Bible Schools at two different locations in the city while another team ministered in two different convalescent homes.

It rained off and on most of the week. Thursday, however, stands out. According to the weather forecast, it was supposed to rain all day. That was the day the team painting the two-story house was supposed to start painting and the team putting in the sidewalk was supposed to pour concrete. The rain, of course, would not be conducive to finishing either of these projects.

I emailed Sandy telling her this. She then sent an email to several ladies asking them to pray. A dear friend, Donna, responded to Sandy's email and said she had asked God to put an umbrella up over Fairmont.

It was raining when we got up in the morning. As soon as the teams got to their worksites, it quit raining. The teams worked all day without any rain, and as soon as they got back to camp at the end of the workday it started raining again. God did put up His umbrella. I told the teams this story before my sermon Thursday evening and it seems like no one doubted that God did have His umbrella over the city of Fairmont, just as Donna had asked him to do.

Hallelujah!

Chapter 79: Blessed From Start To Finish November 2023

I got back last week from teaching for a week in Uganda. I'd known for several months when I was going and what I was going to teach. I taught "The Person and Work of the Holy Spirit." It consisted of 15 classes, three a day for five days. The Lord also gave me opportunities to preach five times, as well as to even lead a Bible study on my way to the airport as I left Uganda to return home. One of the sermons was to a radio audience of about 1.5 million people. This certainly highlights my responsibility to be biblically accurate in my message.

God graciously blessed my trip from start to finish in many ways. Since I was traveling alone with no other Americans, I prayed that God would provide me with someone to travel with. He did that, not only once, but three different times.

The first was when I boarded the plane in Atlanta, headed to Amsterdam. A lady sat next to me, and as we began talking, I learned that she was not only a Christian but she and her husband had moved to another city to be near a church belonging to the Presbyterian Church in America (PCA)—my denomination. She loved Ligonier Ministries and had even gone to a Ligonier Conference. We even had some prayer together when we hit some bad turbulence as we neared Amsterdam; she was extremely fearful of the turbulence and welcomed my suggestion that I pray for our safety.

God provided a second time while I was standing in line getting ready to board my flight from Amsterdam to Kampala. I noticed the man standing beside me in line had a T-shirt on that said "Cedarville University" on the front of it. I asked him about it, and he said that not only did he graduate from there but so did his children. As we continued talking, I learned he was also going to Uganda to train pastors. And not only that—he and the gentleman traveling with him were also PCA. The man I was speaking to was an elder in his congregation while the other man was a pastor. I was blessed to have a couple of conversations with them as we flew from Amsterdam to Kampala.

The third instance was on my flight from Amsterdam to Atlanta on my return trip. This time was another lady seated next to me. She was also a Christian and had been on many mission trips throughout the years. She had recently moved and found a church she liked that she thought was PCA. She knew for sure it was Presbyterian, and while she wasn't really familiar with the various Presbyterian denominations, she thought her new church was PCA.

A concern for me when traveling to Africa is always my health. Let's just say that all systems were a "go" the whole time, and I only had minimal problems that lasted for a couple of hours.

One of my emails to Sandy while I was gone simply explained "God is making disciples." The students' last task before taking the final exam was to write a one-page paper on what they learned throughout the week. Here are representative examples of what they said that confirm the disciple-making that had taken place:

"Since the Holy Spirit is the best teacher, comforter and He is God, I want Him to be my friend and my all in all." (Aita)

"This knowledge helps me to not separate the Holy Spirit from God as a different God and I can also help my people understand this truth." (Rogers, pastor)

"I will let people know that without being born again you cannot enter the Kingdom of God." (Isaiah, pastor)

"Since salvation is God's free gift given to me, I cannot lose it. This has come to me as the best encouragement in the course." (Tamale)

"I learnt that the Holy Spirit cannot dwell together with an evil spirit, so a Christian cannot be demon possessed. I must tell my church members this." (a pastor)

"In the beginning the Holy Spirit was there even before the creation of the world, so He must be respected." (Faith)

"I learnt that the Holy Spirit was even in the Old Testament." (Olupoi, pastor)

"I believe more believers are going to be set free in the Lord Jesus when I freely share with them that they are assured of their salvation and nothing can take it away." (Tamale)

"I have learnt that spiritual gifts are given by God and are to be used for His glory." (Musani)

"It is through the preaching of the gospel that the Holy Spirit brings people to salvation. Our job is to preach the gospel. The Holy Spirit convicts people of sin and brings people to Jesus through faith and repentance." (Ekisa)

Yes, indeed! God graciously blessed this trip from start to finish. I am extremely grateful, not only for all of His answers to prayer and His many blessings, but also for the privilege of being used by Him to make disciples in East Africa.

Closing Thoughts: Abundant Life

Re-reading all of the *God In My Life* testimonies before sending them to my family has been good for me. It has caused me to remember God's gracious faithfulness to me throughout my life. It also brought back fond memories and encouraged me that He is who He says He is in His Word. All of His promises are true!

One of those promises dates back to my conversion on Nov. 7, 1971. I wrote about this in the first *God In My Life* entitled "Becoming A Christian, 'More Than Existing.'"

My goals growing up were two-fold—to become a Marine and to get a tattoo so everyone would know I was a Marine. That being the case, I enlisted in the Marine Corps after high school rather than go to college. For the first year or so in the Marines I felt as though I was just existing. I graduated from basic training on Dec. 4, 1970, and reached my goal of becoming a United States Marine. Only 33 of our original 90 recruits graduated on time without being recycled or tossed out before completing boot camp. I was very proud to be one of them. I then graduated first in my class at my military school and subsequently was meritoriously promoted ahead of others. Clearly, I was getting off to an incredibly good start in the Marine Corps. Yet even with those successes, I felt empty on the inside. I always had to be looking forward to something—going on leave to see Sandy and other family, the next payday or maybe the weekend. I couldn't just get up in the morning and say, "Today is worth living. There is a purpose for me today." The word that kept going through my mind was *existing*. I would tell myself, "Rich, all you're doing is existing." I think this is what Saint Augustine was talking about when he said, "Our souls are restless, O God, until they find their rest in You."

In God's providential timing, I was assigned to Iwakuni, Japan, and met CPL Jerry Henderson; Jerry was a Christian. He shared John 10:10 with me where Jesus said, "I am come that they might have life and have it more abundantly." I thought about Jesus' words, and they spoke to me. As I did so, it seemed as though Jesus said He would give me something that was 180 degrees different from what I had been experiencing. I couldn't think of anything more the opposite of existing (what I was experiencing) than abundant life (what Jesus promised to give me). So, on Nov. 7, 1971, while sitting in a chapel pew during an evening service, I silently prayed, "Jesus, you said you'd give me an abundant life. I want it."

While I understand it doesn't happen to everyone, and conversion experiences differ, I immediately had a sense of being forgiven and cleanliness I'd never experienced before. I knew I'd become a Christian.

What happened that night changed my life and my eternity. My life took a much different direction than it would have otherwise. Had I not become a Christian, I likely would have either re-enlisted in the Marine Corps or gone back to Western Pennsylvania, settled down, gone to college, and become either a biology or Spanish teacher.

I have learned a lot about what having an abundant life means. The NIV translates the Greek word as “have life and have it to the full.” Strong’s Concordance writes that it means “more, greater, excessive, abundant, exceedingly.” HELPS Word-Studies further explains by saying it means, and is used to describe, “beyond what is anticipated.”

I like that—"beyond what is anticipated.” This is, without a doubt, true of my life—and in more ways than I even know. During the last 50-plus years, I have been able to do things and be used by God in ways I never could have imagined. Below are some highlights:

Sandy and I started our married life on totally different wavelengths, since I was a Christian and she wasn’t. True to the promise He gave me on Sept. 28, 1974, He did, indeed, save her and she is now a mature Christian woman, a serious student of God’s Word, and loves coordinating and leading Bible studies for ladies. God has given me two sons who continue to walk with Him, as well as two daughters-in-law who are also Christians. My two grandsons are doing the same and growing in their knowledge of Scripture and hopefully in their walk with the Lord.

God has given me the opportunity to preach the Gospel in several states and in many different countries, including a combat setting in Iraq. He's given me the chance to evangelize and disciple soldiers, and others, and help them grow in their walk with Jesus Christ. I've been able to train chaplains in (or from) several different countries and teach biblical truth to pastors in Uganda and Rwanda. In other words, I've had a ministry that is beyond anything I ever anticipated.

He has blessed us with godly friends, from all over the U.S. and in many countries around the world, whose lives and words are an encouragement to us. There are countless people we can call if we need to pour out our hearts to someone or need prayer. We have friends, both much younger and much older, who would help us or welcome us into their homes if needed. What a blessing they all are.

Thinking of life that is "beyond what is anticipated, a life that exceeds expectations," I think of my military career and the traveling I've done. When I enlisted in the Marine Corps at the age of 18 and left for basic training, I was hoping and praying to make it through boot camp. Making it through wasn't a sure thing, and I knew this. I never could have imagined when I enlisted in the Marine Corps as a private hoping to make it through boot camp that, years later, I would retire as a full-bird colonel in the Army. As I look at my assignments, the people I worked for and with, and my promotions, I see the sovereign hand of God very clearly. In the same way I'll never understand why He chose me for salvation, I'll never understand why He chose to bless my military ministry the way He did. My time in the military was clearly beyond anything I anticipated.

I love to travel, and God has repeatedly given me the opportunity to do so. As I write this, I've been to 49 countries outside the U.S. This still boggles my mind. Again, another example from my life that has far exceeded any expectations I ever had. Even more, I'm sure He has answered an innumerable number of prayers that I'm not even able to recognize, as He answered them behind the scenes without me even being aware—only eternity will reveal all that He has graciously done.

So, Jesus promised me an abundant life. Has He delivered? That's a resounding "Yes!" He has been considerably more faithful to me than I have been to Him. He has done all He said He would and so much more. Soli Deo Gloria!

Acknowledgements

This book would not be possible were it not for the Sovereign and Faithful God I've written about in these pages. I can say with David in Psalm 23 that "The Lord is my Shepherd; I shall not want" and also with Jeremiah's words that "The steadfast love of the LORD never ceases; his mercies never come to an end; they are new every morning; great is your faithfulness."

I cannot thank Him enough that He has proven these words to be true in my life over and over again; more times than I know; even to an undeserving sinner like me. Thank you, Lord!

I am also grateful for the team He brought together for such a project – my family. As you'll see below, with the different interests and skill sets we all have, it was a perfect fit for writing and self-publishing a book.

My deep appreciation goes to Sandy, who I met in first grade. We married when I was 20 years old, and she was 19. She's lived the events of this book with me. She remained totally committed to me and our marriage during the hard times and has been there to celebrate the good times. Not only did she proofread this manuscript and make valuable suggestions, but more importantly than anything having to do with the book, she has blossomed into the "fruitful vine within my house" I wrote about in chapter four. Her hunger to learn God's Word and see other women studying it is exemplary.

The idea to put these testimonies into a book came from our oldest son, Casey. I appreciate so much his suggestion. He has also researched the self-publishing possibilities and developed our timeline for doing so. His expertise in project management kept us focused and on track despite competing demands in all of our lives. This wouldn't have happened without his leadership.

Our youngest son Kelly, as the senior executive editor of a national magazine was the perfect person to serve as my editor for the book. I sincerely thank him for his hours of proofreading as well as providing editorial guidance that proved to be invaluable in bringing the book to fruition. The professionalism he brought to this task was praiseworthy. I couldn't imagine doing this without his expertise.

Soli Deo Gloria!

Made in the USA
Columbia, SC
17 June 2024

36803861R00137